HOW TO MAKE NIGERIA THE GREATEST COUNTRY IN THE WORLD

SUNDAY ADELAJA

Sunday Adelaja
HOW TO MAKE NIGERIA THE
GREATEST COUNTRY IN THE WORLD

ISBN 978-1-908040-87-9

www.goldenpenpublishing.com

Cover design by Alexander Bondaruk
Interior design by Olena Kotelnykova

HOW TO MAKE NIGERIA THE GREATEST COUNTRY IN THE WORLD — Milton Keynes, UK:
Golden Pen Limited, 2017

TABLE OF CONTENTS

INTRODUCTION

Unbuckling my seat belt, I moved to carry my hand luggage and immediately walked through the aisles of the airplane into the arrival lounge of the airport. Once I stepped into the main hall of the airport, everything seemed different, in fact the air seemed to smell differently. This was not a surprise as this is home. Boldly written on one of the boards staring at passengers was 'WELCOME TO NIGERIA'.

In my entourage were people from Ukraine, Russia, Sweden, Germany, Spain and America. On stepping out of the airport, some of the Ukrainian delegates led by my premier disciple Pastor Natasha were hell bent on finding the Nigerian soil. One of the delegates who is an African came to report to me that something strange was happening with our Ukrainians. I went to have a talk with Pastor Natasha and the team and I asked them why they we looking for Nigerian soil. It is dangerous here, don't leave the team, as foreigners, you could attract attention to yourselves I warned.

Their response was as firm as my warning. These group of guys and ladies were bent on kneeling down to kiss and pay homage to the Nigerian soil. Moreover they were actually packing with them as a memorial a part of the Nigerian soil to take back to their countries as a lifelong sign of gratitude and appreciation to what this soil of Nigeria has given to them.

The whole Murtala Muhammed international airport, Lagos Nigeria was stunned by this white people who were kneeling down and kissing the soil of Nigeria. To the crowd of Nigerians that surrounded them, they gave the explanation. You Nigerians don't know what you have. Your land has given birth to sons that have come to bless our nations: Ukraine, Russia, Germany, etc. You are one of the greatest nations on earth.

Thanks to your son, referring to Pastor Sunday, we that are here today came to the knowledge of the lord Jesus Christ. Our lives were saved, our nations redeemed and hope restored to our people. The least we could do is come and pay tribute to the land that gave birth to such great sons like Pastor Sunday Adelaja. Little did they know that Pastor Sunday is just one out of such sons given to the world by this peculiar nation called Nigeria.

No doubt sons like this from Nigeria are numerous. Nigerians who were given birth to either in Nigeria itself or by Nigerian parents are ruling the world in every sphere imaginable. These people are now scattered all over the globe making impact and making a difference in different spheres of the society.

If descendants of Nigeria are making such a difference in the nations of the world, how much greater feats could be accomplished by millions of Nigerians who are back at home. There is no excuse under the sun why Nigeria cannot become the greatest nation on earth. Hence the reason behind this book. On one hand I want to introduce you to a new player on the world stage, on the other hand I want to wake up the sleeping giants in every single Nigerian, as many as will come across this book.

On the particular scene I described above, I made to greet a few people I met at the airport in the language that was familiar with them. I just love everything about this place called Nigeria. Most importantly, I love the people of Nigeria. Their warmth, their personality and the sense of purpose that an average Nigerian seems to carry with him was something I cherished a lot. Nigerians are naturally ambitious people, they have got a lot of resilience and can withstand unthinkable hardships and difficulties. Nigerians are like the palm tree, 'they bend, but they don't break'. No wonder, a lot of them are leaders in different parts of the world.

That for many people has been an irony over the years. It is confusing to find Nigerians leading conveniently in many parts of the world and yet Nigeria itself is undeveloped. As a matter of fact, Nigeria is still regarded as a third world country whereas her sons and daughters are the bedrocks on which the developed countries build their own civilization. What could be happening? What could have gone wrong?

It is a well-known and well-read fact that a Nigerian Dr. Osatohanmwen Osemwengie is responsible for building drones for the American army and he is an integral part of the United States Armed forces. He is among many other Nigerians on which vital components of the United States' economy and national life is built. How can a nation have such a son, yet be struggling to survive?

The feeling I had on this particular occasion is the same feeling I have always had whenever I visited Nigeria.

No doubt, Nigeria is like an undiscovered and untapped gold mine. So much wealth in one place, yet the realities of the people is poverty, hunger, lack and many other problems. What immediately came to my mind was a picture from the scriptures which said,

> WHEN HE (JESUS) SAW THE CROWDS, HE HAD COMPASSION ON THEM, BECAUSE THEY WERE HARASSED AND HELPLESS, LIKE SHEEP WITHOUT A SHEPHERD...
>
> MATTHEW 9:36

I believe that the time for Nigeria to manifest her true greatness has come. In this book, I have laid out a blue print to tapping the enormous wealth and potential of the Nigerian people. I have exposed in this book how to move Nigeria from her current pitiable state to her rightful enviable place. Using facts, statistics and a good chunk of her history, I have unraveled why I think Nigeria is the greatest country in the world, and yet can actualize that potential conveniently. Nigeria by potential could be ahead of America, Germany, France, United Kingdom and other first world countries. I have shown in this book how we can work that potential till we become the greatest single nation on earth.

Do not think that this is impossible until you read this book. You will discover that I am not just making strange statements. Our history and certain events of our recent past also shows that Nigeria can indeed teach America and the rest of the world. Like I said, we have not just been one of the greatest countries in the world in our history, we have achieved global feats recently, and in no distant future, we will again become the greatest country in the world.

I congratulate you for having such a timely book as this in your hand. For together, we will build a nation of our dreams. Welcome to the new Nigeria, welcome to the new world, a world where indeed Nigeria is the leader and the greatest country.

If you believe this and want to learn how this can be made possible, then turn the pages.

For the Love of God, Church and Nation
Sunday Adelaja.

CHAPTER ONE

THE FOUNDATION FOR MY AUDACITY

I know it sounds like fantasy or a fairytale when I say that we can Make Nigeria the greatest country in the world, but this is the kind of fairy tale that could soon become a reality. Many people often ask me for the reason behind my audacity on Nigeria. Many people have asked me why I am always saying such 'big things' about Nigeria. I know perhaps it was your curiosity that also made you pick up this book. You are wondering how I could say 'We want to make Nigeria the greatest country in the world'.

Is it because I'm a Nigerian? But not every Nigerian says such things. Is it because I believe in Nigeria so much? Oh Yes, but much more. What then is responsible for my audacity in saying *'Nigeria is going to become the greatest country in the world'*? We will soon get into the heart of our discussion and you will agree with me no less.

Why Nigeria is Potentially a Greater Nation than America

In this book, I am going to give you concrete facts and figures on why I strongly believe Nigeria is potentially a greater Nation than any other nation on earth including America, perhaps not in today's reality but in the reality of the future. I am also going to outline roadmaps, guideline, plan, and strategies with which we can actualize our potential.

There is no doubt that you will be convinced as much as I am that Nigeria indeed is a greater Nation than the United States, Germany, France, or any of such celebrated countries. Hence the need for all these countries to also learn from the tutorship of Nigeria in some areas, especially in specific areas where Nigeria is currently leading the world.

I am not just saying all of what I am saying as prophecy, I am saying what I know and what I am sure of. I am absolutely convinced of this, and towards this course I dedicate the remainder of my existence on earth. There will be no sweeter story than Nigeria becoming a greater nation than the United States. There will be no better or more classic irony than when all the nations on earth travel down to Africa, to the continent that was once called the Dark Continent, and to the nation on the bank of the Niger River, to learn how to build a nation from grass to grace. Within my lifetime, it is possible that governments of countries will come to Nigeria to learn systems and how to make things work. This will happen when they see how Nigeria dramatically changed the course of her story. Yes, it is possible and this is what will happen soonest.

As far as I am concerned, it is for the future. A future which we can make great and glorious by our united actions and invincible benevolence towards one another. Under no circumstance shall we be drawn again into the experiences of the past, which would have been forever gone, irredeemable and irreparable.

Obafemi Awolowo

Why am I so sure? Am I just declaring a prophecy? What is this that I am talking about? I am not just talking and declaring prophecy. I am speaking from the mountain top. I have seen how things can work, I have in my mind a blueprint to cause and bring about the change that we desire. Hence, my goal and passion for writing such a book as this.

This book will definitely be invaluable to every Nigerian. Beyond Nigerians, everyone who loves their country will have to read carefully to understand the different principles which I will unveil through this chapter and subsequent chapters, so that they might be able to apply similar principles to build their own countries too.

I have no doubt within me, that the reason we are not yet having many developed countries, especially in Africa is because we do not know how to. Now that I think there are many agitations for the development of Nigeria in many quarters, now that many more people seem to be speaking out, something tells me that Nigeria might be finally ready to maximize her potential as a country. Nigeria might be finally ready to teach the rest of the world how to grow a nation.

Hence, my readiness to release unto people that which I am certain of and to give to Nigerians our road map for actualizing true greatness.

At this point, let us consider a few facts quickly.

The power and Resources of America

The United States of America, the most powerful nation on earth, which controls one quarter of the world's economy, stands so tall that it doesn't look possible for an African nation to be able to teach them anything, at least in the near 100 years. Anybody who has been to the United States or lived there would tell you that their colossal status in the world is not by accident. Surely, America is a great nation.

Let's check out some statistics about the United States of America:

America is the father of our modern democracy.

America was the first to put a man on the moon.

Coca-cola, the world's most known soft-drink product comes from America.

America created the modern movie industry Hollywood.

America is the mother of the modern day technological age: Microsoft, Google, Yahoo, Apple, Internet, Facebook, Twitter etc.

America is a land of opportunities and equality.

America is a country of religious liberty.

They are the inventors of the airplane through the Wright Brothers.

The American dollar is the most popular and most traded currency in the world.

America has produced the highest amount of Nobel Prize Winners in history – 270

I can guess what is going on in your mind. What is Pastor Sunday after? How is this guy going to write his way out of this? How is he going to support his statement of when Nigeria teaches America? Ok, here we go.

History Proves it: Nigeria Teaches America

Let's start with the event of recent times. James Entwistle is an American Ambassador to Nigeria. After being an observer and a witness at Nigeria's general elections in 2015, he made a remarkable statement that could signal to the greatness Nigeria possesses as a nation.

Despite our inadequacies and failures, even in that concluded elections, the Hon. Mr. Ambassador still made this compelling statement.

"I am very impressed by the decision of INEC to use technology in this election. The Permanent Voter Cards are very high-tech, they are more high tech than my voter card from the state of Virginia in the US. My voter card does not have biometric. It does not have my fingerprint. The high-tech gives the process more integrity. I congratulate INEC on taking the part of High-tech. I think we need to come and study it so that we can use it in my country."

> Could this be the proverbial cloud in the sky in the shape of a man's hand that made Elijah to outrun King Ahab's chariot?
>
> 1 Kings 18:44, 46

Brethren, I see a picture of things to come for our beloved nation. Somehow I can see afar off, a day when Nigeria would arise as the leader of the black race, that will one day outrun the technologically advanced nations of the first world including America.

Again, I strongly believe that this is not just possible in potential but it is possible in reality. Just as I have shown above by the honest remarks of the honorable ambassador.

Mr. James Entwistle might not have had this in mind when he simply pointed out a visible fact during Nigeria's last election, but beyond the visible, God sometimes allows us to perceive in the spirit things that are to come.

If I will borrow some words from the famous Martin Luther King's speech, **'I have a dream'**, then I will also declare that I have a dream.

I have a dream that one day our nation (Nigeria) will rise up and live out the true meaning of its creed: One nation bound in freedom, Peace and Unity

I have a dream that one day on the red hills of Plateau the sons of Muslims and the sons of Christians will be able to sit down together at the table of brotherhood.

I have a dream that one day even the state of Borno, a state sweltering with the heat of injustice, sweltering with the heat of terrorism, will be transformed into an oasis of freedom and justice.

I have a dream that our little children will one day live in a nation where they will not be judged what tribe or part of the nation they hail from, but by the content of their character.

I have a dream today.

I have a dream that one day, down in the southern state of Bayelsa, little boys and girls of the Ijaw tribe will be able to join hands with little boys and girls from the Fulani tribe of the north.

I have a dream today.

I have a dream that one day every valley shall be exalted, every hill and mountain shall be made low, the rough places will be made plain, and the crooked places will be made straight, and the glory of the Lord shall be revealed, and all flesh shall see it together.

This is our hope. This is the faith that I go back to my country with. With this faith we will be able to hew out of the mountain of despair a stone of hope

(Paraphrasing Martin Luther King's I have a dream speech)

See the Handwriting on the Wall

Dear friends, let it be known to you today, that one day all Nigerians will be able to go back with confidence to their native towns and villages knowing fully well that a new Nigeria will arise. We will go to Kaduna, we will go to Ore, we will go to Sapele, we will go to Maiduguri, We will go to Auchi, we will go to Ilorin, we will go back to the savannas of our northern cities, knowing that somehow our current situation can and will be changed. Nigeria will be a great nation again. Can you see the handwriting on the wall?

To anyone that has ears, let him hear today that America would eventually be referred to as the SETTING SUN, while the most populous black nation on earth would soon be referred to as the RISING STAR.

Is that not already happening? You may doubt, but for anyone who has the eyes of the future, then the handwriting on the wall is quite clear for all to read.

Glimpses of this truth abound for those who have eyes to see. Allow me to share with you some of those facts that are already visible for everyone to see.

A case in example is the way and manner which the deadly virus Ebola was curtailed on the shores of Nigeria in 2014. This was aptly reported in an Online forum called, 'The conversation'.

Ebola - Nigeria Taught the World on Disease Control

The diagnosis of the first case of Ebola in Lagos, Nigeria in July 2014 set off alarm bells around the world. The fear was that it would trigger an apocalyptic epidemic that would make the outbreaks in Liberia, Sierra-Leone and Guinea, where 1322 cases were reported and 728 people had died within five months, pale in comparison.

This fear was very justifiable. Lagos has a population of over 21 million with a population density in built up areas of about 20 000 people per square kilometer. In some areas it is as high as 50 000 people per sq km.

But within three months, the most densely populated country on the continent had managed to contain the deadly virus with only eight deaths. By October 20 the World Health Organization declared Nigeria Ebola free. In stark contrast, fourteen months after the first case of Ebola was declared in Liberia, the country celebrated the announcement that it was Ebola free.

A combination of factors enabled Nigeria to contain the virus in such a short space of time. These included fast thinking on the part of government, a tried and tested tracking system, pooled expertise and assistance from national and international agencies.

The Game Plan

The disease was brought into the country on July 20 by Patrick Sawyer, a Liberian-American financial consultant. Sawyer initially denied exposure to Ebola. He was treated for presumed malaria after suffering from a fever, vomiting and diarrhea.

Sawyer died five days after his arrival. By then he had triggered a line of exposure. By September 2015, 20 people had been infected. Twelve of whom were in Lagos state and eight in Rivers state. Seven more subsequently died.

In the week that Sawyer was diagnosed, an emergency operation center was set up. At its core was the system Nigeria had developed for its war against polio and lead poisoning. The deputy manager of the polio campaign was brought in to head the Ebola response team and operations were rapidly scaled up.

The success of the system laid in a strong coordinating team that supervised house-to-house surveillance. A team of 40 trained epidemiologists and 150 contact tracers was mobilized. They drew up a list of all Sawyer's contacts and those of the subsequent Ebola cases. Locations were mapped and hot spots identified. Fifty teams of contact tracers did house-to-house, in-person visits within a radius of each Ebola contact. In total, they visited 26 000 households in Lagos and Rivers States.

Aside from an initial case assessment, the team also managed the data, infection alerts and rumors, and implemented community-based surveillance.

Five other units backed up their work. These included strategy and coordination, case management and infection control, social mobilization, laboratory services and points of entry.

The strategy team coordinated the activities of the ministries of health and the international partners, dealt with the media and ensured funding, administrative and logistic support. The social mobilization team worked on advocacy, dealing with issues of stigma, the psychological and social well-being of contacts and the reintegration of discharged patients into their communities.

All ports of entry were monitored. The temperature of everyone passing through airports, seaports and land borders were checked for potential exposure.

The case management and infection control team treated and managed every laboratory-confirmed or suspected case. Their job was also to prevent the infection being transmitted. This involved training health care workers at treatment centers and health care facilities on how to take precautions and set up screening centers. They also focused on ensuring safe burials.

In the hours and days following news of Sawyer's diagnosis, fear, myths and rumors spread around Nigeria like wild fire. Much of this was fanned by the press. This led to health care workers refusing to treat any bleeding or feverish patients.

The strategy team brought things under control by engaging the media, communities and key opinion leaders. A multi-pronged plan was put in place. Health care workers in communities were given hands on training about standard precautions and infection prevention. Protective equipment was also made available to health care centers in the communities.

Simple messages were developed that considered the available resources at health care facilities. In some instances, it was as basic as placing a chair at the end of a hospital corridor and cordoning off an area so that suspected cases could be isolated from other patients.

There was also a concerted effort to educate the media and to keep people informed. Daily briefings on patient recovery helped reduce fear.

Despite the tragedy, the Ebola outbreak proved how important it is to rapidly respond to an outbreak with a unified plan, backed up with expertise, manpower and a health system with effective infection controls.

How Nigeria Taught the World

Apart from the massive steps highlighted above, very important was the lesson in national unity evident in the unprecedented co-operation between the Nigerian public and private sectors, teaching hospitals, universities and volunteers. It was a massive team effort led by Nigerians assisted by the international agencies. Nigeria proved the pundits wrong.

The way and manner in which Nigeria managed the deadly disease was a big lesson to the world on disease control. The whole world watched in amazement as Nigeria did the impossible. The deadly disease of Ebola was brought to an abrupt end in just three months, a feat deemed impossible.

Now, only few challenges in the world are as posing and deadly as the Ebola virus. I personally believe that the Ebola virus is as deadly if not more deadly than the virus of corruption, nepotism and ethnicity, insecurity and myriads of others eating the country deep. Now, who says Nigeria cannot end all of this same way it put an end to Ebola in just three months. This is a feat only a country as determined and resolute as Nigeria can achieve.

Do you now see a reason why I said that Nigeria will be referred to as the RISING SUN in a short while?

So impressed was the rest of the world by this giant effort by Nigeria that the World Health Organization Director-General Margaret Chan, came out to say *"If a country like Nigeria, hampered by serious security problems, can do this, ANY COUNTRY IN THE WORLD experiencing an imported case [of Ebola] can hold onward transmission to just a handful of cases."* She declared this at a time noting that even the United States had no Ebola control yet. Oh, what a nation I belong to, my beloved Nigeria.

Also the United Nations Council and several governments of Nations poured encomiums on Nigeria, praising her for providing leadership for the world in disease control.

Nigeria, Not America is World's Police

Apart from providing leadership for the world in the area of disease control, a little known fact to many people in the world today is that Nigeria, not even America is the Police of the world with her unrelenting commitment to peace keeping missions around the world.

As at 30th June, 2017, Nigeria has a total of 1667 men of the armed forces in the United Nations peace keeping troops, a report available on the United Nations website. America has only 74 men of the armed forces in the Peace keeping operations of the United Nations.

The strides and commitment of Nigeria to keeping world peace is one that cannot be downplayed. This is a major way that Nigeria is providing leadership for the world.

Nigeria first provided UN peacekeepers to Congo (ONUC) from 1960 to 1964. Since then, Nigeria has been an active participant in UN peacekeeping missions, deploying military contingents, unarmed military observers, military staff officers, formed police units, police advisors and civilian experts to over 25 UN missions. Nigeria is currently one of the largest UN contributing countries with military and civilian personnel deployed in ten UN peacekeeping operations and the African Union Mission in Somalia

Nigeria has also played pivotal roles in other non-UN missions in Africa. As the preponderant power in West Africa, Nigeria has been the main provider of military and other resources for ECOWAS peace operations to the tune of US$8 billion in its various missions in Cote d'Ivoire, Guinea-Bissau, Liberia, Mali, and Sierra Leone.

During the peak of the Liberian and Sierra Leonean civil wars in the 1990s, Nigeria provided over 70% of ECOMOG's military and civilian personnel, as well as logistical support. In 2003, it deployed 1,500 troops to the ECOWAS Mission in Liberia (ECOMIL), and a medical and signals team to the ECOWAS Mission in Cote d'Ivoire in 2003 (ECOMICI). In 2004, 1,500 Nigerian troops were deployed in Darfur as part of the AU Mission in Sudan (AMIS). Recently, Nigeria also provided 1,200 troops to the African-led International Support Mission in Mali (AFISMA), and 200 police officers to AMISOM. Nigeria deployed the first set of individual police officers (IPOs) in Africa in ONUC in 1960 while the pioneer Formed Police Unit (FPU) of 120 officers was deployed in Liberia in 2004.

While the rest of the world applauds this initiative by Nigeria, it is rather sad that many Nigerians are ignorant of the large efforts the country is making. Many people do not know that the stability of the world is largely dependent on the backing the United Nations receive from the Nigerian troops who have been described as some of the best fighting forces on land around the world.

This is historic. This points to the future. A future where Nigeria leads in all things. The actions of successive Nigerian governments is applaudable in this regard. More concerted efforts only need to be geared towards International operations, not forgetting the security concerns of her citizens at home.

I know you will readily agree with me that if Nigeria through her troops can strive towards Peace keeping and stability of many countries around the world, nothing stops her from squashing all security threats and terrorist threats within her borders in a few time. This has been so difficult over the years because many acts of terrorism within Nigeria are largely politically motivated. This acts of terrorism have never brought the capability of our military force to the fore. We only need to dismantle the interests of the powerful forces who sabotage the efforts of the government and Nigeria will be one of the most peaceful countries in the world. The Nigerian armed forces have boasted time and again of their capability to stem any act of terrorism within days only if every political interest and motivation is removed from the equation. Such is the power of the country called Nigeria. A nation that does not cower under threat. A nation that does not break in spite of war.

In fact historically, many people have thought that Nigeria would be a country forgotten immediately after the Civil war that occurred from 1967 to 1970. A period in time when almost a million lives were lost.

The Nigerian Civil War, also known as the Nigerian-Biafran War, was a three-year, bloody conflict with a death toll numbering more than one million people. Having commenced seven years after Nigeria gained independence from Britain, the war began with the secession of the southeastern region of the nation on May 30, 1967, when it declared itself the Independent Republic of Biafra. The ensuing battles and well-publicized human suffering prompted international outrage and intervention.

Carved out of the west of Africa by Britain without regard for preexisting ethnic, cultural and linguistic divisions, Nigeria has often experienced an uncertain peace. Following decades of ethnic tension in colonial Nigeria, political instability reached a critical mass among independent Nigeria's three dominant ethnic groups: the Hausa-Fulani in the north, Yoruba in the southwest, and Igbo in the southeast. On January 15, 1966, the Igbo launched a coup d'état under the command of

Major-General Johnson Aguiyi-Ironsi in an attempt to save the country from what Igbo leaders feared would be political disintegration.

Shortly after the successful coup, widespread suspicion of Igbo domination was aroused in the north among the Hausa-Fulani Muslims, many of whom opposed independence from Britain. Similar suspicions of the Igbo junta grew in the Yoruba west, prompting a joint Yoruba and Hausa-Fulani counter-coup against the Igbo six months later. Counter-coup leader General Yakubu Gowon took punitive measures against the Igbo. Further anger over the murder of prominent Hausa politicians led to the massacre of scattered Igbo populations in northern Hausa-Fulani regions. This persecution triggered the move by Igbo separatists to form their own nation of Biafra the following year.

Less than two months after Biafra declared its independence, diplomatic efforts to resolve the crisis fell apart. On July 6, 1967, the federal government in Lagos launched a full-scale invasion into Biafra. Expecting a quick victory, the Nigerian army surrounded and buffeted Biafra with aerial and artillery bombardment that led to large scale losses among Biafran civilians. The Nigerian Navy also established a sea blockade that denied food, medical supplies and weapons, again impacting Biafran soldiers and civilians alike.

Despite the lack of resources and international support, Biafra stood firm refusing to surrender in the face of overwhelming Nigerian military superiority. The Nigerian Army however continued to slowly take territory, and on January 15, 1970, Biafra surrendered when its military commander General Chukwuemeka Odumegwu Ojukwu fled to Cote d'Ivoire.

During this civil war, an estimated 3,000 to 5,000 people died daily in Biafra from starvation as a result of the naval blockade.

The international reaction to the military conflict in Nigeria at the time helped define how the world now views and responds to similar crises. Even in conflict, Nigeria still taught the world.

The war became a defining point for many Nigerians. This is why I believe that in spite of the current agitations and tensions in the country, a good student of history knows that Nigeria has been through worse yet remained indivisible and invincible.

This is also the reason I challenge us as Nigerians to accept our fate and common destiny. We were created to be together and nothing can ever set us apart. The beauty of Nigeria is in her diversity. A thing is only as beautiful to the degree of her diversity. Beautiful paintings often come in many colors. Even the rainbow is not monochrome.

So quick was the recovery of Nigeria after the civil war that it became stronger economically than the now celebrated United States and England.

In 1976, 75 kobo exchanged for one British Pound and 60 kobo exchanged for one US dollar. Can you imagine that? A nation that had just been through tragic war rose back within a space of about five years to become one of the strongest economies in the world at that time. What that currency exchange meant was that if you had one thousand dollars at the time, you only had six hundred naira, and only 750 naira if you had a thousand pounds. This was just four decades ago.

It is unfortunate what the naira is today, but out of the ashes I see a beacon of hope. I see Nigeria rising again through the woods. If in just forty years, so much devastation and degradation happened, then in less than forty years, we can rebuild every ruin. We can make Nigeria the greatest country in the world again.

At this period in 1976, a holder of the Nigerian passport could travel to more than a hundred countries without visa. Nigerians were looked on with respect at airports and around the world. Our embassies around the world were filled with people who wanted to come visit Nigeria for a trip of their lifetime. Nigeria was the golden spot.

If you are old enough, you will remember the FESTAC 1977, a period when the entire world beamed its light on Nigeria. It was a celebration of art and culture, unity and diversity. It was too much of a beauty to behold that the entire world at the time struggled to be in Nigeria. The world trooped down to Nigeria. The world simply had never seen anything like that celebration before and Nigeria showcased what has been regarded as the largest art festival in the history of the world.

Festac '77, also known as the Second World Black and African Festival of Arts and Culture (the first was in Dakar, 1966), was a major international festival held in Lagos, Nigeria, from 15 January 1977 to 12 February 1977. The month-long event celebrated African culture and showcased to the world African music, fine art, literature, drama, dance and religion. About 16,000 participants, representing 56 African nations and countries of the African Diaspora, performed at the event. Artists who performed at the festival included Stevie Wonder from United States, Gilberto Gil from Brazil, Bembeya Jazz National from Guinea, Mighty Sparrow from Grenada, Les Ballets Africains, South African Miriam Makeba, and Franco Luambo Makiadi. At the time it was held, it was the largest pan-African gathering to ever take place.

A housing estate known as Festac Village was constructed as accommodation for about 17,000 participants. However, the long-term objective of the village under the Federal Housing Program was to relieve some of the housing pressure in Lagos. The housing estate was proposed for construction within two years, with more than 40 contractors working on different sites of the project. In total 5,088 dwelling units were built prior to the festival and an additional 5,687 were to be completed by the end of 1977. During the festival, the housing estate was the venue for performance rehearsals and interaction by participants as various troupes rehearsed their routines in the day and at night.

For hosting the performances and lectures, a state-of-the-art multipurpose theatre was built, to serve also as a lasting center of African art and culture. The theater's design was based on the Palace of Culture and Sports in Varna, Bulgaria, with the Bulgarian firm Technoexportstroy hired to build it. The then new complex had two exhibition halls, a 5,000-capacity performance and event hall, a conference hall with 1,600 seats and two cinema halls. The theatre hosted dance, music, art exhibitions, cinema, drama and the colloquium.

All of those facilities at the time were some of the best in the world. Today, these facilities lie in ruins.

How then did Nigeria fail and fall from such enviable heights? How did we get into the dust that we are in today? Well, this will be the subject of another of my book titled 'WHY COUNTRIES FAIL'. It will be an intellectual look into the cause of every Nigeria's problem. However, that is not the focus of subject right now.

How can Nigeria rise again to become the greatest country on earth? That is our focus. Just as we rebuilt Nigeria after the civil war to have bigger and stronger economy in just five years than even the United States and England, we need to rebuild our country again. You and I only need to take on this pressing challenge, we need that same determination that got us out of the war and dispute, to build a country not just for ourselves but also for our children.

We need to go back to such unity as was displayed during FESTAC '77, where humanity was not about race or tribe or gender. It was about the one thing that unified all of us; We are one black race, we are one nation, indivisible under God.

Looking to the Future

Let's consider another area in which Nigeria is bound to lead the world. Nigeria's population was just 16 million in 1911. It is projected to hit 444 million by 2050, surpassing the US and becoming the 4th largest country in the world. If it continues at that growth rate, in another 25 years, it is expected to be the largest country in the world.

Lagos' population in 1872 was 60,000. By 2050 it will be the third largest city in the entire world with a current population of over 21 million people.

What does this spell for Nigeria? It means standing tall when it comes to human resources in the world. It means we will have many more Nigerians breaking grounds. If we will only take advantage of our enormous human capital and provide the environment for each citizen to thrive, Nigeria will easily become the greatest nation on earth.

In the next chapter, I am going to continue on this all important discussion of making Nigeria the greatest country in the world. I am sure that at this stage of the book, you already know that nothing is wrong with Nigeria, we have been among the greatest country in the world in times past, we can do it again.

Let us consider more steps for the actualization in the next chapter.

NUGGETS

- Now that there are many agitations for the development of Nigeria in many quarters, Nigeria might be finally ready to maximize her potential as a country.
- Despite our inadequacies and failures, even in 2015 concluded elections, the US Ambassador admitted to the superiority of Nigeria's voting card.
- Somehow I can see afar off, a day when Nigeria would arise as the leader of the black race, that will one day outrun the technologically advanced nations of the first world including America.
- America would eventually be referred to as the SETTING SUN, while the most populous black nation on earth would soon be referred to as the RISING STAR
- The way and manner in which Nigeria managed the deadly Ebola disease was a big lesson to the world on disease control.
- A little known fact to many people in the world today is that Nigeria, not even America is the Police of the world.
- The international reaction to the military conflict in Nigeria during the civil war helped define how the world now views and responds to similar crises.
- So quick was the recovery of Nigeria after the civil war that it became stronger economically than the now celebrated United States and England.

CHAPTER TWO

NIGERIANS TEACHING THE WORLD

Previously, we looked at the achievements of America as a great nation. We also considered few among the many achievements that Nigeria has made historically. We compared the tales of the two nations and we evidently diagnosed that nothing, absolutely nothing is wrong with Nigeria.

We established the fact that what Nigeria is going through currently is a phase in her national life. This phase is bound to usher in a new phase of industrialization and massive development.

I will now show you examples of Nigerians who are already showing the world the greatness in Nigeria. Let us look at certain Nigerians who are demonstrating that indeed Nigeria can become the greatest country in the world.

Showcasing Nigeria's Prowess

A big news hit the news rooms of the world media in the first quarter of 2015. Stars were born. Munira Khalif from Minnesota, Stephan Stoykov from Indiana, Victor

Agbafe from North Carolina and Harold Ekeh from New York got multiple admission offers in all eight Ivy League schools in the United States of America: Brown University, Colombia University, Cornell University, Dartmouth College, Harvard University, University of Pennsylvania, Preston University and Yale University.

This type of feat is recorded yearly in the United States of America. A semester before, Kwasi Enin, 17, a Ghanaian immigrant attained the same height. Still a few years earlier another Nigerian prodigy Saheela Ibraheem, attained the same height and ended up going to Harvard at 15. She is regarded as one of the 50 smartest teenagers in the world. She was treated to a dinner by no less a person than the President of the United States himself Barack Obama.

What makes this story of interest today is that, of the four outstanding students that year, TWO OF THEM ARE NIGERIANS, while all four are immigrants. Victor Agbafe and Harold Ekeh where born to Nigerian parents. This goes to prove my point that Nigeria is the rising star of the future world. While the fact that all the prodigies are immigrants shows that America is taking a nose dive and is becoming the setting star of the future.

Harold Ekeh - a Prodigy

Harold Ekeh's family moved to the United States from their native Nigeria when he was 8. He's done pretty well for himself since then.

Ekeh, a senior at Elmont Memorial High School in Long Island, New York, had a GPA of over 100 at school, he got a 2270 (out of 2400) on the SAT, and he was accepted to all 13 colleges he applied to, including all eight Ivy League schools, as well as Johns Hopkins and MIT.

Ekeh was also a Model U.N. leader, a drummer, a youth choir director and a leader at a mentorship program at his school. *"My parents' hard work and my hard work finally paid off,"* Ekeh, 17, told the New York Post.

Elmont's principal, John Capozzi, told CNN that Ekeh is *"one of the most humble young men I've ever had the opportunity to meet."*

"Anybody who sees my story can say, 'If he can do it, I can do it,'" said Ekeh. *"I'm just a kid who had a real strong support system."*

With such exceptional young men like Harold Ekeh, tell me why I won't boast that Nigeria can again become one of the greatest countries in the world. Think of how many of such fine young men we have in our dilapidated classrooms all across Nigeria today just waiting for the perfect environment for them to thrive to blossom like Harold Ekeh.

If Harold never got a chance to travel out of Nigeria, he perhaps would have been forgotten and would not have become a world star, but the chance and opportunity he got showed the 'Nigerianness' in him. It showed that Nigerians when given the right soil and nutrition and environment, will grow to become the largest cedar in the forest.

What our government must immediately strive to do, what we all as Nigerians must do as a matter of urgency is to create a better learning environment for all of our young ones. There is no doubt that what we greatly owe the younger generation is access to good education and a chance to life.

We must as a matter of emergency provide this opportunity. There is no doubt that even if this will be the only agenda of our government and their only pursuit, we will well be on our way to become the greatest country in the world today.

There is no argument that hidden in this young people lies the discovery and solution to our power and energy problems, this young minds will solve our problems of healthcare, these young people will revolutionize agriculture and find solutions to the problems of our environment. These young people will become our armed forces and solve our pressing security problems. Such is the power of the Nigerian mind. I believe that the Nigerian given the right environment will always do better than any other person from across the world. This is how to make Nigeria the greatest country in the world.

Let us look at another exceptional Nigerian in the story named Victor Agbafe

Victor Agbafe – Making Nigeria Proud

Victor Agbafe was born to Nigerian parents. Agbafe applied to 14 colleges - all eight Ivies, as well as other top schools such as Stanford, Duke, and Emory - receiving acceptances to each one.

"If you look at the acceptance rates of these schools, it's just so difficult to get into even one," he said. *"So I would have been happy at any one of them."*

"It wasn't about that I did this, it was a positive thing for my family, my school, my community," Agbafe said.

Still, he had advice for other high school students who might want to accomplish the same feat.

"Life is a roller coaster ride, and if you keep trudging forward and put forth your best effort, things are going to end up the way they should," Agbafe said. "Always stay positive, stay focused, stay humble, stay hungry - those are the keys to success."

At Cape Fear Academy, Agbafe served as Student Body president, played on the basketball team, and participated in various other extracurricular activities.

The 17-year-old planned to become a neurosurgeon after he finishes college and medical school, eventually going into public policy. To this end, Agbafe said he was looking for a school with strong government, economics, and science programs.

He wants to explore questions such as *"how can I use the platform for treatments, how can I make it available for everyone in all communities."*

Like few other high school students who gained acceptance letters to all eight Ivies, Agbafe is a first-generation American; his mother came to the US from Nigeria.

"I just feel that there's a strong sense of the opportunity available to us," he said. *"Our parents remind us that there have been a lot of people before us who have had to make a lot of sacrifices."* Victor told Business Insider.

Victor's story like Harold's showcases the latent potential of Nigerians.

I dream of that day when we will have an educational environment like the United States currently has, then we will unleash on the world millions of young men like victor Agbafe and Harold Ekeh. The world has not seen anything yet, through such young men, Nigeria is again poised to become the greatest country in the world.

Victor and Harold are not alone in their giant strides, such achievement is fast becoming a yearly routine for Nigerians living in America.

Augusta Uwamanzu-Nna - Proud to be Nigerian

Augusta is another Nigerian-American who made headlines in 2016 when she achieved same feat as Victor and Harold, getting accepted into all the 8 Ivy league schools. It was only the second year such a feat was achieved and on both occasions, it was done by Nigerians.

Daily mail reported Augusta's story exclusively as these:

"For the second time in as many years, a student at suburban New York's Elmont Memorial High School has been accepted at all eight Ivy League universities.

Augusta Uwamanzu-Nna had to decide whether she'll attend one of the prestigious northeastern universities. The daughter of Nigerian immigrants also could choose from Johns Hopkins University, Massachusetts Institute of Technology, New York University and Rensselaer Polytechnic Institute.

'My recent accomplishments reflect the hardworking ideals of the town of Elmont, my supportive parents and my dedicated teachers. I am elated but most importantly I am thankful,' said the 17-year-old valedictorian with a 101.64 weighted grade-point average.

Augusta is the daughter of Nigerian immigrants, who are obviously thrilled with her application success.

'My family is so excited,' Augusta told News 12 Long Island. 'Sometimes I feel like they get so much more excited

than me. They literally scream. When I called my mom and told her, she was screaming on the phone.'

'Though I was born here in America, I visited Nigeria many times,' she told WABC. 'And I've seen that my cousins don't have the same opportunities that I have. So definitely, whatever I do, I want to make sure that it has an impact on Nigeria."

Please read carefully the later part of Augusta's story. This young lady carefully attributed her success to the opportunities she got in the United States. She knew that there wasn't anything special about her and that her relatives in Nigeria could have done same if they were given same opportunities. When given same chance, all her cousins and nephews could have achieved same feat too.

She has a mission to impact Nigeria, to bring change to the country and to provide opportunities for people.

If a young girl as Augusta is making this claim, then what is stopping our government? Our privileged citizens? Our elite? Our politicians? What is stopping you and I?

If we all can focus our energy on just creating a better environment for our young people alone, Nigeria will become the greatest country in the world.

Ifeoma White-Thorpe-Yet Another Prodigy

Just in the early parts of 2017, another Nigerian-American high school student, Ifeoma White Thorpe achieved the rare feat of being accepted into all of the Ivy League universities in the United States, yet again.

Seventeen-year-old Ifeoma of New Jersey was accepted to all eight of America's elite Ivy League universities, including Harvard, Yale, Columbia, UPenn, Brown, Cornell, Dartmouth, and Princeton, according to ABC7.

In high school, Ifeoma was the student government president. She first made headlines in 2015, when she won accolades for an essay, entitled "Let Freedom Ring", which she wrote and read for the National Liberty Museum's "Selma Speech & Essay Contest" to mark the 50th anniversary of the epic Selma March.

Ifeoma, a senior at Rockaway's Morris Hills High School, said she aced her advanced placement courses but she never expected to be accepted by all eight universities which was something almost extra ordinary to do.

The achievements of these young Nigerians become more incredible when you realise that even American kids are not able to perform such feats. American kids themselves do not have admission into their own schools, the 8 Ivy League schools. A feat which is almost synonymous to Nigerian and symbolic of Nigeria.

This is enough proof of Nigeria's ability to become the greatest in the world. When we choose to invest in our tomorrow, in our young people, then there will be no country as great as Nigeria on the surface of the earth.

I am an individual who is actively campaigning and advocating that the bulk of our national budget and expenditure should be spent to train our young people. There is no doubt that when this is done, many more of Ifeomas, Victors, Augustas and Harolds will emerge from Nigeria. Nigeria will have the greatest amount of scholars the world has ever seen. Nigerians will win the Nobel Prize like child's play, there will be many inventions of Nigerian origin and businesses will spring forth from all corners of the country.

Hear Their Cry

This is a cry to our government. This is a cry of the young people. Can you hear their cry? They are saying to save their future. There is a future in every child, there is a genius in every Nigerian kid just waiting for the right environment to manifest it. Every Nigerian kid just wants an opportunity.

In a later part of this book, I will share my personal story. You will discover that I was just another Nigerian Kid whose future could have been buried if I never got the scholarship to travel to Europe at the age of 19. In fact, if I never got the small money to pay for my certificate education at the end of my secondary school, I would probably still have been a farmer in my village today. Do you understand this point?

Nigerian young minds are not just stirring the waters of America in the United States, similar feats is being achieved in the United Kingdom too. Nigerians are proving that in any given any location and the right environment, they will surely emerge as the best and the leader. Such is the case and example of Enatarari Kalango. In fact, of the eight best results achieved in the 2016 Cambridge examinations conducted across the world, three of those were by Nigerians namely Ayodeji Oluwafisayo, Ukabiala Chimdi and Kalango Enatarari.

Enatarari Kalango - Acing Cambridge Easily

She received the prestigious award for her exceptional performance in the June 2016 Cambridge examinations.

Enatarari won the prize for the Best across Eight Cambridge IGCSEs in the Cambridge International Examinations conducted across the six continents of the world in June 2016.

The international qualifications are recognized by the world's best universities and employers as giving students a wide range of options in their education and career.

The award ceremony, which held at the Intercontinental Hotel Lagos on May 19 2017, was designed to recognize Outstanding Cambridge Learners in 2015 and 2016 and the partner schools that have exemplified Equality, Diversity, Inclusion (EDI) and Child Protection policies.

Enatarari achieved all A-stars (A*) in nine of her IGCSE subjects; (English, Mathematics, Biology, Geography, Literature, Business Studies, Economics, History and ICT). She was also the Valedictorian 2016 having obtained the highest GPA in her Year Group. In her Cambridge Checkpoint examination in June 2014, Enatarari got the highest attainable score in all her subjects (English 6.0, Mathematics 6.0 and Science 6.0).

Speaking on the award, Enatarari thanked her parents; saying, "*my base of support was and still is my family. They prayed for me, motivated me and reassured me that I could be the best. Knowing that I had parents who tailored every decision they made for my good, how could I not strive to make them proud?*"

She also credits her school's boarding house, noting, *"they created a system where peers worked together to better each other, and improvements were rewarded at the same time as pushing us to try harder."*

She said, *"I am finishing my first year of A-levels in England. Next year, I hope to be accepted to the University of Cambridge to study Economics. I want to thank my parents, my brother and Meadow Hall. I believe my success at IGCSEs was the start of a streak, with many more to come."*

Enatarari is another face of the Nigerian future. She boldly represents the kind of potential present in Nigerian kids.

See the Nigerian Future

At this stage of the book, I wish to emphasise that in another 15 years, all of these bright minds that have been acknowledged in this book will just be in their prime, ready to deliver the greatness in them fully for the benefit of the world. Many of them will just be a little above thirty years. This will be a great opportunity for Nigeria to tap into the enormous power of these great minds.

Nigeria must not repeat the mistakes of the last forty years when she suffered brain drain and lent some of her finest sons and daughters to many countries of the world to develop. Nigeria must now strive to retain the best among her own people for the benefit of the nation.

In a few years, among these young people and the numerous other kids like them will be researchers, scientists, literary giants, etc. These are the set of Nigerians that will bring home the laurels including the Nobel Prize. Nigeria will then sit comfortably in the comity of achieving Nigerians.

We only need to do the right things and take the right steps. With this kind of brilliant minds, we can become that country with the highest number of Nobel Prize winners in the world.

There is no doubt that the zeal of young people like Augusta can be tapped into, who wants to work to impact her country. There is no doubt that many young people are like her, each person wanting to create better opportunities for the rest of Nigeria and the rest of the world.

Not only are these young people doing incredible things overseas and winning all the laurels, we have many more beautiful Nigerian minds who are blazing the trails in world's universities. Nigerians are leading the world in the sphere of education. Here a few examples of such men.

Nigerians in Top World Universities

Dehlia Umunna - Leading from Harvard

Dehlia Umunna is an outstanding Nigerian-born American lawyer and lecturer who is a Clinical Professor of Law at Harvard Law School.

A release on the Harvard website about her appointment says she has been a lecturer at Harvard Law School (HLS) since 2007, and is Deputy Director and Clinical Instructor at HLS's Criminal Justice Institute (CJI), in which she supervises third-year law students in their representation of adult and juvenile clients in criminal and juvenile proceedings and arguments before Massachusetts' Supreme Judicial Court and Appeals court.

Before joining Harvard Law School, Umunna was a trial attorney with the D.C. Public Defender Service and an adjunct professor of law and Practitioner in Residence at the Washington College of Law, American University. She currently serves as a faculty member for Gideon's Promise, and is a frequent presenter at Public Defender trainings across America.

She was a board member of the District of Columbia Law Students in Court Clinic and was a guest lecturer for several years at the George Washington University Law School.

She is the author of the article "Rethinking the Neighborhood Watch."

Dehlia at this pinnacle clearly demonstrates the excellence of Nigerian minds. She shows that the mind of the Nigerian is not in any way inferior, rather Nigerians possess what it takes to lead the world.

Ilesanmi Adesida - Uncommon Physicist

Ilesanmi Adesida (born 1949, Ifon, Ondo State, Nigeria) is a naturalized American physicist of Nigerian descent.

He is the Donald Biggar Willett Professor of Engineering, former Dean, College of Engineering, since 2007, a member of the board of Fluor Corporation.

In May 2012, the Board of Trustees of the University of Illinois selected Adesida to be the next vice chancellor for academic affairs and provost of the Urbana campus; a position he has held since August 15, 2012.

Adesida's field of academic research is nanotechnology with special emphasis on high speed devices used in communications. He has held posts as director of the Center for Nanoscale Science and Technology, director of the Micro and Nanotechnology Laboratory, professor of materials science and engineering, professor of electrical and computer engineering, professor of the Beckman Institute for Advanced Science and Technology and research professor of the Coordinated Science Laboratory, all at the University of Illinois. Adesida earned his bachelor's (1974), master's (1975), and doctoral (1979) degrees in electrical engineering from the University of California, Berkeley.

Adesida is an expert in the processing of semiconductors and other materials at the nanometer-scale level and in ultra-high-speed hetero structure field-effect transistors - the sort of transistors used in cell-phones, fiber optics communications, deep space communications, and other applications. His contributions have provided insights into the limits of advanced lithography and other nanofabrication techniques.

He and his students continue to work in the areas of Nano electronics and high-speed opto- electronic devices and circuits. His recent work has focused on the development of devices and circuits in the key materials such as indium phosphide and gallium nitride utilized in high-performance, wireless, optical fiber communications, and high temperature applications. He has published over 250 refereed journal papers, over 180 conference papers and presentations, and many books.

Adesida is a Fellow of both the Institute of Electrical and Electronics Engineers (IEEE), the American Association for the Advancement of Science(AAAS), the American Vacuum Society, and the Optical Society of America.

Again, Adesida is a confirmation that Nigerians are some of the cornerstones upon which many developed nations have built their foundations. Can you imagine what will happen if Nigeria chooses to use some of these illustrious sons and daughters as bedrock of her own achievements. What is more interesting that brilliant minds like Adesida exist in no small measure among Nigerians.

Let us take a look at another example.

Kunle Olukotun - Designing for the Future

Kunle Olukotun is a Cadence Design Systems Professor, of Electrical Engineering & Computer Science at Stanford University and he has been on the faculty since 1991. Olukotun is well known for leading the Stanford Hydra research project which developed one of the first chip multiprocessors.

Olukotun founded Afara Web systems to develop high-throughput, low power server systems with chip multiprocessor technology. Afara was acquired by Sun Microsystems. The Afara microprocessor technology, called Niagara, is at the center of Sun's throughput computing initiative. Niagara based systems have become one of Sun's fastest ramping products ever. Olukotun is actively involved in research in computer architecture, parallel programming environments and scalable parallel systems.

Olukotun currently co-leads the Transactional Coherence and Consistency project whose goal is to make parallel programming accessible to average programmers. Olukotun also directs the Stanford Pervasive Parallelism Lab (PPL) which seeks to proliferate the use of parallelism in all application areas. Olukotun is an ACM Fellow (2006) for contributions to multiprocessors on a chip and multi-threaded processor design. He has authored many papers on CMP design and parallel software and recently completed a book on CMP architecture. Olukotun received his Ph.D. in Computer Engineering from The University of Michigan.

Olutokun is a Nigerian giving the world a feel of the possibility of Nigeria becoming the greatest country in the world. His efforts are land breaking and shows that the point of this book is not off the track. Indeed, Nigeria can become the greatest country in the world.

Toyin Omoyeni Falola - Keeping steps with History

Toyin Omoyeni Falola (born 1 January 1953 in Ibadan) is a Nigerian historian and professor of African Studies. He is currently the Jacob and Frances Sanger Mossiker Chair in the Humanities at the University of Texas at Austin.

A Fellow of the Nigerian Academy of Letters, he is the author of numerous books, including Key Events in African History: A Reference Guide, Nationalism and African Intellectuals, and many edited books including Tradition and Change in Africa and African Writers and Readers.

He is the co-editor of the Journal of African Economic History, Series Editor of Rochester Studies in African History and the Diaspora, and the Series Editor of the Culture and Customs of Africa by Greenwood Press. He has received various awards and honors, including the Jean Holloway Award for Teaching Excellence, the Texas Exes Teaching Award, and the Khaldun Distinguished Award for Research Excellence.

Like Toyin Falola, we have many more Nigerians winning global awards and clinching world-wide fame. Nigerians can truly become the best at whatever they set their minds to. Hence, I am convinced that if we set our minds to make Nigeria the greatest country in the world, we can achieve it.

Peter P. Ekeh

Peter P. Ekeh went to the University of Buffalo's African American Studies as Professor in 1989. He was Chairman of this department from 1993 to 2001. Before going to Buffalo, Dr. Ekeh taught at the University of California, Riverside (1970-73); Ahmadu Bello University, Zaria, in northern Nigeria (1973-74); and at the University of Ibadan, Nigeria (1974-1989). He was Chairman of the Department of Political Science at the University of Ibadan (1978-1983) and Chairman of the Ibadan University Press (1983-1988).

Peter Ekeh received his undergraduate education at the University of Ibadan (1961-64) and his graduate degrees in sociology from Stanford University (1965-66) and University of California, Berkeley (1966-70).

Dr. Ekeh's early research interest was in sociological theory, in which he published Social Exchange Theory: The Two Traditions (1974), and in psychoanalytic theory. He has since developed special interests in African politics and history, in which he has some leading publications. Dr. Ekeh's article "Colonialism and the Two Publics in Africa: A Theoretical Statement" (1975) is one of the most cited publications in the field of African studies.

Peter Ekeh has held several fellowships in Europe, United States, and Japan. He was a Fellow of the Woodrow Wilson Center for International Scholars, Washington, D.C. (1988-89). Dr. Ekeh has received various research and scholarship awards in Nigeria and the United States.

Ekeh is a proud Nigerian who showcases the very essence of excellence of the Nigerian spirit. It is indeed possible for Nigerians to excel everywhere they find themselves. It is not only Dr. Ekeh who shows this to be true. Isidore Okpewho as well.

Isidore Okpewho

He is a University of New York Distinguished Professor of Africana Studies, English, & Comparative Literature at Binghamton University.

Born in Nigeria, Isidore Okpewho has a B.A. in Honors Classics from the University of London, a Ph.D. in Comparative Literature from the University of Denver, and a D.Lit. in the Humanities from the University of London. He has taught at the State University of New York at Buffalo (1974-76), University of Ibadan (1976-90), Harvard University (1990-91), and Binghamton University (since 1991).

Okpe's areas of specialization are in African and comparative literatures, with a specialist emphasis on comparative oral traditions. His major publications in this field include The Epic in Africa: Toward a Poetics of the Oral Performance (1979), Myth in Africa: A Study of Its Aesthetic and Cultural Relevance (1983), African Oral Literature: Backgrounds, Character, and Continuity (1992), and once upon a Kingdom: Myth, Hegemony, and Identity (1998). His edited scholarly volumes reveal an expansion of his academic interests from oral literature (The Oral Performance in Africa, 1990), to modern African literature.

He completed a book on an African epic under the title Blood on the Delta: Art, Culture, and Society in The Ozidi Saga, as well as working on a new book project African Mythology in the New World. He has also published some four dozen journal and book articles in these areas.

Professor Okpe who is also an active novelist with four titles, The Victims (1970), The Last Duty, (winner of the African Arts Prize for Literature 1976), Tides [winner of the Commonwealth Writers Prize for Africa 1993), and Call Me By My Rightful Name (2004).

Another perspective we can look at Nigerians teaching the world is in the area of this many Nigerian academics providing tutorship in top Universities around the world. It is surely a beauty to behold, a good thing for Nigeria.

While we will work towards creating the educational environment for this academics in Nigerian campuses, it will always be beautiful to see our illustrious sons and daughters shining the sun in Universities around the world.

Mobolaji E. Aluko

Mobolaji E. Aluko (born 2nd April, 1955; in Lagos, Nigeria) is a professor of Chemical Engineering at Howard University, Washington, DC, and was Chairman of its department from 1994-2002. With a BSc degree (1976) in Chemical Engineering from the University of Ife (Nigeria; now Obafemi Awolowo University), he also attended Imperial College, University of London; University of California, Santa Barbara; and State University of New York, Buffalo (for graduate and post-doc studies).

He has had sabbatical teaching and research stints at various times at the University of Washington, (Seattle; Materials Science Department); the University of Maryland (College Park; Chemical Engineering), and the University of Ado-Ekiti (Nigeria; Mechanical Engineering Department). He started teaching at Howard University in August 1984. His research interests are mathematical modeling, chemical reaction engineering, electronic materials processing, energy systems, information technology and education pedagogy.

He is presently President/CEO of Alondex Applied Technologies, LLC: Lead Consultant and International Coordinator of the LEAD Program at the National Universities Commission (NUC) in Nigeria; and Principal Academic Consultant of AfriHUB (Nig.) Ltd., an ICT resource provider for universities in Nigeria.

He is an activist and frequent commentator on Nigerian and African affairs.

It is commendable that Mobolaji Aluko is not just an Academic in diaspora, he is lending his voice to the Nigerian Affairs. I want to encourage many more Nigerians in diaspora to lend their voice to the issues of Nigeria and consider a way of giving back to the society that produced them.

The exposure and the experience that these Nigerians in diaspora have will go a long way in helping us build the nation of our dreams.

Dr. Peters

He is Professor of Petroleum Engineering at the University of Alberta, Canada.

Dr. Peters has served on the faculty since 1980. He has four years of industrial experience and specializes in fluid flow in porous media. His research interests include application of advanced imaging technologies for the physical and mathematical modeling of fluids in porous media. Dr. Peters has published more than 70 technical articles and reports.

His recent Research Projects include Computer Imaging in Enhanced Oil Recovery, Numerical Modeling of Laboratory Flow Experiments, Numerical Modeling of Fluid Flow and Transport in Porous Media Assisted by X-Ray Computed Tomography and Nuclear Magnetic Resonance Imaging.

He has won Honors such as the Frank W. Jessen Professor in Petroleum Engineering, George H. Fancher Professor in Petroleum Engineering among others.

While Petroleum remains a dwindling source of the Nigerian economy, there is no doubt that newer technologies being developed by these illustrious son of Nigeria, Dr. Peters, the gains of Nigeria in oil can be maximized.

Abba Gumel

Abba Gumel is a Professor in the Department of Mathematics and the Director of the Institute of Industrial Mathematical Sciences (IIMS) of the University of Manitoba. He received his B.Sc. and Ph.D. degrees from Bayero University (Kano, Nigeria) and Brunel University (London, England) respectively. His main research interests are in (i) Mathematical Biology, (ii) Nonlinear

Dynamical Systems and (iii) Computational Mathematics.

The main objective of his research work is to use mathematical theories and methodologies to gain insights into the transmission and control dynamics of human diseases of public health interest. He has supervised a number of research students and postdoctoral fellows. Professor Gumel has been the coordinator of the Mathematical Biology Team of the IIMS since its inception in 1999, and represents the University of Manitoba on the Board of Directors of the Fields Institute for Research in Mathematical Sciences, Toronto.

Professor Gumel is an active member of the Canadian Applied and Industrial Mathematics Society (CAIMS). In addition to serving on its various committees earlier, Professor Gumel was elected Secretary of CAIMS from 2007-2009 (he was re-elected for a second term: 2009-2011). Professor Gumel is also a member of the Canadian Mathematics Society (CMS) and serves on the Outreach Committee of the Society for Mathematical Biology (SMB). Owing to its interdisciplinary nature, Professor Gumel's work enjoys fruitful collaborations with mathematical and medical scientists from around the world. Professor Gumel has received series of awards and he is listed among the top African Mathematicians of the 1990s on the website of the Mathematicians of the African.

This is a big source of pride for Africa and Nigeria in particular. One would expect that Abba Gummel would be more celebrated within his own country than outside the shores of the country.

This is a challenge to the Nigerian government to immediately begin such sons and daughters that have raised the Nigerian flag so high for the world to see.

Apart from the yearly National awards, we need to create special awards for Nigerians in diaspora who are doing so well to bring Nigeria pride in the comity of nations.

Godwin Chukwu

Godwin Chukwu is a Professor at University of Alaska, USA.

Dr. Chukwu has worked for the firms of Elf Petroleum, Petroleum Associates of Lafayette, Agip Energy and Natural Resources, in different engineering and professional capacities. He has taught both undergraduate and graduate engineering and related economics courses at the University of Port-Harcourt Nigeria, and currently the University of Alaska Fairbanks. In addition, he has taught several short courses in fluid hydraulics and hydrodynamics, and drilling optimization, as a consultant. He served as the chairman of the petroleum engineering department at UAF from 1992-1995 and 1996-2002.

Dr. Chukwu has authored and co-authored over 65 research publications in the areas of drilling, hydraulics, gas-to-liquids transportation, petroleum geology and natural resource utilization. He is internationally known for his work in the area of non-Newtonian fluid hydraulics applied to oil well drilling/production technology, and hydrodynamics of GTL transportation in pipes. His current research work in gas-to-liquid transportation and operational challenges through the Trans-Alaska

Pipeline System is sponsored by the US Department of Energy, and supported by Alyeska Pipeline Service Company.

Dr. Chukwu is a registered professional engineer in both Nigeria and the state of Alaska. He has served in several professional bodies and organizations which include the Society of Petroleum Engineers (SPE) and the Accreditation Board for Engineering and Technology (ABET). Dr. Chukwu served as the UAF Faculty Senate President-elect (May 2001-May 2002), and subsequently, the Faculty Senate President (May 2002-May 2003).

Dr. Chukwu is another Nigerian who has shown capability to turn around the fortunes of Nigeria through engineering feats.

Why must these Nigerians be put to use by the rest of the world, yet Nigeria herself hardly see how to maximize the capabilities of her own sons and daughters? I believe that this has to change.

Prof. Raymond Akwule

Prof. Raymond Akwule has more than 25 years of teaching, research, and project planning and implementation experience in the fields of telecommunications and information technology as well as Mass Communication and Media studies at George Mason University in Fairfax Virginia USA.

He is the author of Global Telecommunication: The Technology, Administration and policies (Butterworth-Heinemann). This book has been used as text in several major Universities in the USA and worldwide. He is also the author of numerous articles and conference presentation.

He was Director of Center for Telecommunications Information and Broadcasting, which later become the Center for Media Research and Telecommunications at the department of Communication, George Mason University. He was one of the founders of the MA Telecommunications programs at the same university.

Professor Akwule has advised many countries in the area of Media and communication and has spearheaded the design and implementation of several nation's ICT networks as well as e-government, e-commerce and e-education programs in Africa.

If a Nigerian has written textbooks which is being used in several Universities in the United States, then Nigeria can indeed become the greatest country in the world.

PROF CHINEDUM OSUJI

He is an associate professor of chemical and environmental engineering at Yale University.

According to the Yale University website, Prof. Osuji's interests are centered on the physics and physical chemistry of soft matter - studying and elucidating self-assembly and basic structure-property relationships of colloids, liquid crystals, polymers and biological materials. Research in the Osuji lab is focused on structure and dynamics of soft materials, i.e. on the relationship between the micro-structure of polymer melts, surfactant phases, liquid crystals and colloidal gels and their dynamics. He works on structure-property relationships in liquid crystalline block copolymers, directed self-assembly of surfactants and polymers, rheology of colloidal gels and microfluidic platforms for studying multiphase flows. His expertise is in electron microscopy, x-ray scattering and rheology. Highlights of ongoing work include the development of self-assembled polymer nanocomposites for use as active layers in organic solar cells, the design of microfluidic mimics of vascular structures for model studies of red blood cell mechanics, and elucidation of shear thickening and aging behavior in particulate suspensions and gels. These efforts have important implications in energy generation, the design of next generation microfluidic bio-assays and the design and processing of complex fluids such as toner inks and cosmetics.

No doubt that Prof. Osuji is an inventor per excellence and his works must be celebrated also in Nigeria. With the support of our government, this man can surely achieve more than he has achieved.

Chukwu Nwakuche Ethelbert

Ethelbert Nwakuche Chukwu earned his B.Sc. in Mathematics at Brown University (1965), a M.Sc. in Applied Mathematics at the University of Nigeria-Nsukka and earned his PhD. in Mathematics from Case Western Reserve University (1972). Thus began a remarkable career in Mathematics Research and Administration.

Dr. Chukwu's first position was at Cleveland State University where he was an Assistant Professor (1972) and Associate Professor in 1976. In 1977 until 1981 he was Dean of the School of Post-Graduate Studies at the University of Jos in Nigeria. He also served as Professor of Mathematics (1978-81) and Chair of the Mathematics department (1979-81). From 1981 until 1984, Dr. Chukwu was Vice Chancellor (President) of Federal University.

From 1984 until 1989, he held several visiting positions at universities in the U.S. However, in 1989 E.N. Chukwu became Professor of Mathematics at North Carolina State University where he remains until today. He has worked on several research projects for NASA since his membership in the faculty of mathematics at NCSU.

Dr. Ethelbert Nwakuche Chukwu was awarded the Griot Mathematics Award by The Academy for Pan African Research and Culture. He has over 75 papers and books on various topics from Classical Analysis to Operator Theory and Applied Mathematics- linear and non-linear differential equations, and Mathematical Economics.

Dr Chukwu is an astute Mathematician who has contributed a lot to the development of institutions in Nigeria. He can only be applauded and challenged for more contributions to his mother land. He has been able to combine international influence with impact on his motherland. Isn't this what Nigeria requires from every Nigerian?

George Ude

Dr. George Ude, a tenured full Professor in the Department of Natural Sciences at Bowie State University is the recipient of the University of Maryland's 2016 Wilson H. Elkins Professorship which honors recipients for teaching, research and service. Dr. Ude embodies the essence of the vision of Dr. Elkins for whom this professorship is named, as enshrined in his famous quote:

> There is nothing more precious than a gifted mind. Our colleges and universities rise above

THE COMMONPLACE WHEN THEY MAKE IT POSSIBLE FOR THE TRULY GREAT THINKERS OF OUR TIME TO NURTURE THE CREATIVE SPIRIT OF OUR YOUTH. THIS IS THE EDUCATIONAL PROCESS AT ITS FINEST.

WILSON H. ELKINS

Dr. Ude is a great thinker whose professional career is devoted to nurturing the creative spirits of our youth.

An excellent teacher, Dr. Ude emphasizes the use of discovery-based pedagogy to facilitate student learning and augment faculty capacity to instruct student. To accomplish this, he secured extramural funding from the NSF to establish a state-of-the-art Genomics Lab to support his course in molecular biology. This enables students to have hands-on experience in the class. He regularly mentors students in his lab to pursue intensive research, some of which result in publication in peer-reviewed journals.

Dr. Ude has established collaboration with internationally regarded research entities such as the DNA Learning Center at Cold Spring Harbor Laboratory, NY, the NIH, and the USDA. These efforts are geared toward diversifying the experiences of students in the STEM disciplines, and provide them opportunities to learn from world class scientists. His most recent grant received from NSF has enabled him to establish a new Applied Biotechnology Course, and also provide international research opportunities to students. In the latter effort, Dr. Ude travels to Nigeria with several students to conduct DNA-Barcoding research, in partnership with Cold Spring Harbor and the Godfrey Okoye University at Enugu, Nigeria. The effort has led to the hosting of two international workshops on DNA barcoding in Nigeria and the US.

Over the past several years, Dr. Ude has conducted the very popular Biotech Summer Institute, to provide hands on experience in molecular biology to college students, high school students, and high school teachers from various parts of the country. Testimonials from participants show that the program has enhanced the teaching and learning of biology, and aided some in gaining admission to graduate programs. His annual Biotechnology Symposium offers students the opportunity to make professional presentations to the public.

Dr. Ude is the faculty coordinator of the Undergraduate Research Program at Bowie State. In 2015, Dr. Ude led the departmental effort to host the first HBCU Course-Based Undergraduate Research Experience (CURE) at Bowie State, attended by about 40 professors from more than 20 HBCUs around the country. Another creative effort geared towards facilitating student learning of biology is the BioMusic project he initiated in 2010. The goal of the effort was to interest the youth in science by communicating in accessible format, by setting biological concepts and process to rap music. On the research front, Dr. Ude's area of interest is plant genomics. He collaborates with scientists from around the world in conducting research on banana (Musa, sp.) to search for alternative model system for polyploidy studies, as well as understanding the developmental components of parthenocarpy in the species using Next Generation Sequencing techniques

It is significant to note that his work always involves students. Journal publications have emerged from this work, as well as several book chapters published by major publishing houses.

Dr. Ude contributes to the service of his profession through various avenues. He is the founder of the International Society of African Biotechnologists and Bioscientists (ISABB), and organization devoted to promoting STEM on the African continent. The organization publishes four Online journals to disseminate scientific knowledge for the betterment of especially Africa. He is also the Editor-in-Chief of the African Journal of Biotechnology.

He has received several awards some of which are: (1) 2008 Exemplary Mentor award, for distinguished scholarly work and support of Science, Mathematics, Engineering and Technology (SMET) domain and the Model Institutions for Excellence Initiative MIE; (2) 2009 Bowie State University (BSU) College of Arts and Sciences (CAS) Faculty Creative award for a faculty member who engages in an activity that may not result in a scholarly publication, but represents an outstanding achievement in his or her profession (BioMusic CD production); (3) 2011 and 2014 CAS Outstanding Faculty award, the highest award in the College of Arts and Sciences which honors a faculty member who has distinguished him/herself as an all-around professional, excelling in research, teaching, service and scholarly or creative activities; and the (4) 2015 Outstanding International Faculty Outreach award that honors a faculty member who engages in significant international activities or sponsors activities that enrich the international experience of students and advance the international mission of the College.

What a Nigerian to be proud of.

With this caliber of men and women in top Universities around the world who are blazing the trails and are Nigerians, I need anyone to convince me against my idea that Nigeria will indeed become the greatest country in the world.

Are you also fascinated by the thought and imagination of having even if it is 50% of this people working within Nigeria? There is no excuse that Nigeria has not to become the best and the greatest.

It must be noted however that the caliber of minds we have in our campuses and Universities across the nation are not in any way inferior. These learned gentlemen and ladies only need to be supported given the right materials to work with and enough incentives for their work.

There is no gainsaying the fact that the world has moved from a technology-based economy to a knowledge-based economy, hence the need for Nigeria to arise rapidly to this modern global trend.

If our country will truly develop and rise to become the greatest country in the world, we must place priority on our gifted minds in our institutions of learning before they also find exit through the nearest embassy.

We must support our scholars, we must give them the opportunities needed that makes them compete favorably with their counterparts from any other part of the world.

We can build our economy on just this robust opportunity of having some of the greatest minds in the world with us same way Stanford University has been used as the bedrock of the outstanding economy of California in the United States.

Another major achievement of Nigerians is in the area of Medicine, innovation and invention.

Let us see some of the landmarks that Nigeria has created for the world through Medicine and invention. Who are these Nigerians?

Nigeria's Global Trail Blazers in Medicine and Inventions

Dr. Ferdinand Ofodile

Dr. Ferdinand Ofodile is a US board certified plastic surgeon. Dr. Ofodile is a clinical professor of surgery at Columbia University, New York. He has been practicing plastic surgery for more than twenty years. He is a Fellow of the American College of Surgeons (FACS), and a Fellow of the American Association of Plastic Surgeons. He is also board certified in general surgery.

Dr. Ofodile received his Bachelor of Science (BS) and Doctor of Medicine (MD) degrees at Northwestern University, Chicago, Illinois. He did his surgical training at Columbia Presbyterian and Harlem Hospitals, New York. He did a Fellowship in Plastic Surgery at Mayo Clinic.

Dr. Ferdinand Ofodile designed a NASAL IMPLANT FOR RHINOPLASTY in Blacks and Hispanics, named the "Ofodile Implant" after his name. The Implants are designed to produce more natural results that fit the black and Hispanic features.

Dr. Ofodile has published numerous scientific articles in plastic surgery and presented scientific plastic surgery papers in many international conferences.

He has received several awards and has been named one of "America's Top Physicians" by the Consumers' Research Council of America and "Top African American Doctor" by the Network Journal.

Dr. Ofodile has led volunteer medical missions to several parts of the world, including the Dominican Republic, Haiti, Nigeria and Mozambique.

A man such rare stature definitely must have his place in restructuring the health sector of his country especially when such a sector lay in shambles.

The diverse specializations of Dr. Ofodile can definitely be used to re-engineer the framework of healthcare delivery in Nigeria.

Dr Rotimi Badero

Dr Olurotimi John Badero has made Nigeria proud after his recognition as the only fully trained and board certified cardio-nephrologist (combined kidney and heart specialist) in the world today.

Dr. Badero is the Executive Director of Cardiac Renal & Vascular Associates, the Medical Director of St. Joseph Hospice, and he is on the global Advisory Board of the therapeutics experts on Thrombosis and Atherosclerosis, Merck Pharmaceuticals U.S.A.

Badero who resides in the United States was born the seventh of nine children to Chief Eliab Olufemi Olujoye Badero and Stella Taiwo Badero and raised in Lagos and Ogun states, Nigeria.

Badero attended St. Mary's Private School Lagos for his primary school education. He received his secondary school education at Federal Government College Odogbolu, Ogun State. He was admitted to the Medical School at Obafemi Awolowo University, Ile-Ife, Osun State.

Following medical school, he completed his internship year at Obafemi Awolowo University Teaching Hospitals Complex at Ile-Ife.

He worked at General Hospital Isolo in Lagos to fulfill his one-year service requirement with the National Youth Service Corps. After this, he relocated to the United States where he completed three years of internal medicine residency training at SUNY Downstate Medical Center.

Badero was accepted at the Emory University School of Medicine in Atlanta where he completed a two-year fellowship training in nephrology and hypertension.

Badero returned to SUNY Downstate to complete a three-year fellowship training in cardiovascular medicine.

Following this, he attended the Yale School of Medicine where he completed a fellowship in invasive & interventional cardiology and another in peripheral vascular intervention.

Badero then returned to SUNY Downstate for a year of fellowship training in interventional nephrology and dialysis access intervention.

In all, Dr. Badero completed an unprecedented 10 years of continuous post- graduate medical training and he is currently board certified and a consultant in:

1. Internal medicine
2. Nephrology & Hypertension
3. Interventional Nephrology & Endovascular Access
4. Cardiovascular Medicine

5. Nuclear Cardiology
6. Invasive & Interventional Cardiology.

He performed the first trans-radial cardiac catheterization and coronary angioplasty at Central Mississippi Medical Center.

Dr. Badero is a recipient of many awards including:

- The Association of Black Cardiologists scholarship award for the Best Cardiology Fellow in the U.S.
- The 2014 Mississippi Healthcare Heroes in the state of Mississippi.
- He was also named one of Jackson, Mississippi's Best Surgeons.

Dr. Badero has authored many peer reviewed journals and he is currently on the editorial board of the International Journal of Nephrology & Renovascular Disease.

Like I have already established so far in this book, breaking new grounds is almost synonymous with being a Nigerian.

There is no doubt that with thousands of young people still in Nigeria with same mental prowess as Dr. Badero, Nigerians will still accomplish many more world-class achievements.

Chidi Achebe

He is currently an assistant professor at Tufts University School of Medicine.

Dr. Chidi Achebe completed undergraduate studies in natural sciences, history and philosophy at Bard College; received an MPH from the Harvard School of Public Health, his Medical Degree at Dartmouth Medical

School and an MBA degree at Yale University's School of Management.

He also completed his residency in both Internal Medicine and Pediatrics at the Texas Medical Center in Houston, TX.

He has held the position of Medical Director at Whittier Street health center, Assistant Professor at Tufts University School of Medicine, and is currently the President and CEO of the Harvard St. Health Center.

After several years of work at various Boston health centers, Dr Achebe now sees *"the struggle against inequalities in health and health care for all vulnerable, underserved Americans, as the next stage of the Civil Rights movement;"* and has dedicated his life's work to helping to solve the problem of health care inequity in America's health care system.

Dr Achebe speaks at youth summits, conventions, conferences, schools, barber shops - focal gathering areas where he can reach underserved patients - reminding the community of the value of health, preventive care, and the quality of service readily available at Harvard Street.

While expanding his unique implementation of **"medicine without borders"**, Achebe works as a passionate advocate for the global community through his writings that call attention to worldwide health concerns such as the HIV/AIDs pandemic and Prostate Cancer.

His efforts have earned him a featured TV appearance on Basic Black; profile in the Boston Globe and AOL Black Voices, an interview on WUMB-FM's Commonwealth Journal; and feature length articles in several international periodicals, journals, and newspapers.

I have told you about all these people for you to realize that amazing talents is in no short supply in Nigeria. Nigeria has a ready tool to work and transform herself.

For all these Nigerians to excel in a very competitive society and environment like America, it goes a long way to point out the potential of our people.

Other Nigerian Inventors And Innovators

Jelani Aliyu

Jelani Aliyu, hails from Sokoto State, Nigeria and is General Motors Lead Exterior Designer and the designer of the Chevy Volt. General Motors is the world's largest automobile maker. The car has been described as an American Revolution and one of the hottest concepts in the design line.

Jelani was born in 1966 in Kaduna Nigeria. The fifth of seven children, theirs was a very close-knit family.

From 1971 to 1978, he attended Capital School, Sokoto, an excellent school and this served as a very productive educational experience for him. In 1978, he gained admission into Federal Government College, Sokoto, from where he graduated in 1983 with an award as the best in Technical Drawing.

After FGC, he got admission into the Ahmadu Bello University, Zaria to study Architecture, but soon discovered that curriculum did not support his future vision and plans.

After considering other institutions in Nigeria and their academic programs, he concluded that only one of them had the study criteria that would support his future goals. The institution in which he chose to pursue his education was one he felt offered the best creative programs and had experience that would give him the best foundation required to study Automobile Design abroad. That institution was the Birnin Kebbi Polytechnic.

He was there from 1986 to 1988 and earned an associate degree in Architecture, with an award as Best All-Round Student. While there, he did some in depth research into home design and construction, looking into materials and structures that would be most compatible with our environment and climate; buildings that would stay cool in a hot environment with little, or no artificial electrical air conditioning. Upon graduation from the polytechnic, Jelani worked for a while at the Ministry of Works, Sokoto.

In 1990, Aliyu moved to Detroit, Michigan to enroll at the College for Creative Studies in Detroit under a Sokoto Scholarship board sponsorship. Having always wanted to study Automobile Design, this was a dream come true and an absolutely fascinating experience. The course was very practical and emphasis was put on creativity and the development of new designs to provide solutions. He received his degree in automobile design in 1994.

In 1994 he began his career with the design staff of General Motors. He worked on the Buick Rendezvous and was the lead exterior designer of the Pontiac G6. He also worked on the Astra with General Motors' Opel Division.

With his brilliant work on the design of the Chevrolet Volt, which was unveiled in 2007, Jelani Aliyu is considered by many to be the super star of the General Motors renaissance.

The efforts of the Nigerian Government to bring Jelani Aliyu back into the country to head the the National Automotive Design and Development Council (NADDC) must be loudly applauded.

The National Automotive Design and Development Council (NADDC) was set up in May 2014 after a merger of previous agencies. Much of NADDC's work has been guided by an automotive policy approved in 2013. The policy mainly aims to boost local car production and reduce vehicle imports.

If Jelani Aliyu's efforts at this agency succeeds, then Nigeria would have gone a long way in diversifying her economy.

This efforts of our government must not stop with Jelani Aliyu, every Nigerian in diaspora of note, especially those that I have mentioned in this book must be given same handshake.

Brig. Gen. Dr. Otu Oviemo Ovadje (Rtd.)

Dr. Otu Oviemo Ovadje born in December 1954 in Delta State, Nigeria, is a highly accredited Nigerian medical doctor who invented the Emergency Auto Transfusion System (EAT-SET): an affordable, simpler and effective blood auto-transfusion system. He pioneered this invention at the Military Hospital Ikoyi Lagos when he was working at the Benin Teaching Hospital and the University Hospital in Lagos.

Auto-transfusion medical mechanism is a technique that has already been in use in developed countries. However it has little to no existence in developing nations due to the fact that it is expensive, complicated to use and requires electricity to work; something that most parts of the African countries are still lacking.

Dr. Oviemo's invention of the EAT-SET is a simpler, inexpensive and more effective compared to the conventional Auto-transfusion technique being used in the industrialized nations.

The EAT-SET system recovers blood from the patient's internal bleeding organs. This device has the ability of using the patient's own blood and in a safe manner reinfuses it into the patient's blood system. This is if the processing is done within 24 hours after hemorrhage. The patient's blood is drawn into a special collection container and later reinfused into the patient by gravity after it has undergone a filtration process. The EAT-SET system takes about 2 minutes to process about 500 ml of blood. The EAT-SET system presented the solution to the problem of blood salvaging from the body cavities and replaced the gauze filtration technique that is being practiced in developed nations, by providing an improved alternative.

Dr. Oviemo's system is completely closed and is manufactured by reusable collection devices that have disposal filters hence there is no risk of infection. It has a suction and retransfusion lines that are connected to the EAT-SET system. It is also fitted with a hand-held vacuum pump that is used for sucking blood from the patient's body cavities. This is the key advantage of the EAT-SET; it functions without electricity, making it the most ideal auto-transfusion system for most parts in Africa that still don't have electricity supply or the electricity is expensive to utilize. In addition to this, it prevents diseases transmissions and avoiding immunological complication associated with homologous transfusion. Another key advantage of the EAT-SET system is that is gives room for greater flexibility in terms of its use and blood supply to blood banks especially in Africa nations where blood resources extremely scarce due to lack of an organized voluntary blood donation programs.

Although Dr. Oviemo started the prototype project with a budget of $120, his invention became quite practical in Africa and addressed the unique challenges facing Africa thereby attracting much attention and recognitions. This led to Dr. Oviemo being declared the best African scientist in 1995, and hence he established the EAT-SET industries. He has since received financial support from United Nation Development Program (UNDP), Nigeria's government and World Health Organization (WHO) which is the acting executing agency and provides assistance as far as coordination of the project is concerned. The EAT-SET has earned Dr. Oviemo various highly accredited awards from World Intellectual Property Organization (WIPO) and the African Union (AU) among other renowned organizations.

Inventions and scientific breakthroughs therefore is not foreign to Nigeria as some may think it is. When many more Nigerians are encouraged into scientific research, Nigeria will rain many more products on the world. Dr. Oviemo is a pace-setter and he must be challenged to reach out to the next generation of scientists and innovators within Nigeria.

Bennet Omalu

Bennet Ifeakandu Omalu was born in Nnokwa,(What city is this from?) Nigeria, in September 1968, during the Nigerian Civil War. The conflict had forced his family to vacate its gated compound in the village of Enugwu-Ukwu, but they were eventually able to return there to resume a comfortable lifestyle.

The sixth of seven children of a civil engineer and a seamstress, Omalu was a shy but gifted student with a fertile imagination. He was admitted to the Federal Government College in Enugu at age 12 and dreamed of being an airline pilot. However, at age 15 he began medical school at the University of Nigeria.

After earning his degree in 1990, Omalu interned at Jos University Hospital, before being accepted to a visiting scholar program at the University of Washington in 1994. He then served his residency at Harlem Hospital Center, where he developed his interest in pathology.

In 1999, Omalu moved to Pittsburgh to train under noted pathologist, Cyril Wecht at the Allegheny County Coroner's Office. He continued his education at the University of Pittsburgh, completing a fellowship in neuropathology in 2002 and a master's in public health and epidemiology in 2004.

While working at the coroner's office in September 2002, Omalu examined the body of Mike Webster, a former professional football player with the NFL's Pittsburgh Steelers. Webster had displayed patterns of distressing behavior before his death from a heart attack at age 50, and Omalu was curious as to what clues the former player's brain would reveal.

After careful examination of the brain, Omalu discovered clumps of tau proteins, which impair brain function upon accumulation.

After confirming his findings with top faculty members at the University of Pittsburgh, Omalu named the condition chronic traumatic encephalopathy (CTE) and submitted a paper titled "Chronic Traumatic Encephalopathy in a National Football League Player" to the medical journal of Neurosurgery.

His discovery shook the world especially the NFL. Omalu is known as a hero of the American Medical Profession. His efforts has been put into the Hollywood movie starred by Will Smith called 'Concussion'.

Along with his position as chief medical examiner for San Joaquin County, he serves as president of Bennet Omalu Pathology, as well as associate clinical professor of pathology at UC Davis Medical Center.

Again Dr Omalu has shown the world that it is possible to be a Nigerian and move the world with discoveries and inventions. His particular stand for the truth despite being pressured by the NFL to withdraw his publication indicting the league is commendable.

He has proven Nigerians are honest and hardworking people.

Mohammed Bah Abba

Born in 1964 into a family of pot makers and raised in the rural north, Mohammed Bah Abba was familiar from an early age with the various practical and symbolic uses of traditional clay pots, and learned as a child the rudiments of pottery. Subsequently studying biology, chemistry and geology at school, he unraveled the technical puzzle that led him years later to develop the "pot-in-pot preservation/cooling system".

He was selected as a Rolex Laureate in 2000 for this ingenious technique that requires no external energy supply to preserve fruit, vegetables and other perishables in hot, arid climates. The pot-in-pot cooling system, a kind of "desert refrigerator", helps subsistence farmers by reducing food spoilage and waste and thus increasing their income and limiting the health hazards of decaying foods. Abba says he developed the pot-in-pot "to help the rural poor in a cost-effective, participatory and sustainable way".

The pot-in-pot consists of two earthenware pots of different diameters, one placed inside the other. The space between the two pots is filled with wet sand that is kept constantly moist, thereby keeping both pots damp. Fruit, vegetables and other items such as soft drinks are put in the smaller inner pot, which is covered with a damp cloth. The phenomenon that occurs is based on a simple principle of physics: the water contained in the sand between the two pots evaporates towards the outer surface of the larger pot where the drier outside air is circulating. By virtue of the laws of thermodynamics, the evaporation process automatically causes a drop in temperature of several degrees, cooling the inner container, destroying harmful micro-organisms and preserving the perishable foods inside.

Abba was a rare young man who proved the tenets of innovation to be true, you can use the resources available in your environment to solve global problems.

This is a challenge especially to the young minds of Nigeria. You do not need an Harvard education before solving problems in your community. You can locate a problem and begin to use the resources in your environment to creatively solve the problem.

Steven Udotong

Steven Udotong, an African-American teenager of Nigerian ancestry, is set to become the first Black high school student to build a nuclear fusor reactor.

Scientists say nuclear fusion holds the promise of providing a waste-free, emission-free, and inexhaustible alternative power source to meet global energy demands.

Udotong, 16, a junior at Cinnaminson High in southern New Jersey, is hopeful that when complete, his energy fusor will be able to drive hydrogen atoms together with terrific force inside a steel orb, fusing them into helium and producing a small amount of energy.

Udotong's nuclear fusion reactor will be a small-scale version of the reaction that takes place in the sun, according to Philly.com.

Unlike the more widespread process of producing energy through nuclear fission, which works by splitting atoms in a nuclear power plant and yields dangerous waste as a by-product, nuclear fusion is a comparatively eco-friendly and incredibly cost effective process of producing energy.

Udotong is by no means the first person to build a fusion reactor - the earliest working model was built in the 1950s by the inventor Philo Farnsworth - but the mini reactor, which he is assembling in the basement of his New Jersey home, will make him the first Black student to build one.

Udotong says that he was inspired to build a reactor in the 10th grade, after his class took lessons on nuclear energy production, *"I grew curious after we flew by the topic of nuclear energy in my chemistry class last year. I decided to do more research, and I soon learned that I could actually make a nuclear fusor."*

Udotong says he undertook further research and learned more about nuclear fusion from Fusor.net, which allowed him to meet and interact with other fusion enthusiasts.

In addition to his mother, Nonye Udotong, a physics instructor at Rowan University who encouraged his interest and actively supported him, Udotong has also enjoyed the support of his four brainy brothers, one of whom assisted him to set up a GoFundMe page to raise more than the $1,000 he needed to build the fusion reactor and help Udotong achieve his dream of becoming the first African-American student to complete such a project.

And Udotong and his brothers were more than successful with their GoFundMe page, where they raised $2,375, effectively exceeding their goal.

According to Udotong, although well-meaning people often voice their concern about the possible dangers of working with a nuclear reactor, there is only a minimal risk (from electromagnetic radiation) involved, most of which can be managed by wearing the appropriate safety outfits.

With Udotong, Nigeria has a bright future in invention and innovation. Imagine what this young man can achieve if he is given the support and recognition that he needs. I have decided to include his name to show the world that Nigeria is coming, and we can indeed become the greatest country in the world.

How Nigeria can have the World's Best Products

The Jews have made an extensive impact in the world. Though a small group of people of people accounting for only about 0.2% of the world, their touch on life is indelible. I will share details of those impacts later.

Soon, I will show you examples of Jews and the impacts that this very small group of people have made in the world. There is a Jewish component in most things we use on a daily basis, from the Personal Computers, Cellphones, drugs, social networks, medical devices, Food, etc. In fact there is probably no home in the world not having something Jewish within it.

Facebook, Goldman Sachs, Oracle, Starbucks Coffee, Toys, Warner Bros, Hasbro, Craiglist, eBay, Levi's Jeans, are Jewish.

Dell, Microsoft, Google, Ralph Lauren, Calvin Klein, GAP, Dreamworks, Bloomberg, Citigroup, are all Jewish too. All of these products mean the Jews can decide to shut down the world as we have it today.

All of this is from a people whose population is not even up to half of Lagos state Nigeria. Their people are not smarter than ours, their brains are not better than ours. What's more? We have the Nigerian spirit going for us. We have Nigerians who have attended same schools with Students of Jewish origin and are better academically. I personally pastor a church that is having a large percentage of Jews. As special and extra ordinary as they are, I know that Nigerians are not worse. In my university days with over sixteen thousand students, we had thousands of Jews yet by the grace of God I was able to outperform all of them as a Nigerian and as a black person. There is nothing special, it only takes hard work and I am sure Nigerians can work hard. Nigerians can turn things around and contribute to the world to make it a better place. We can indeed be the greatest nation on earth, hence my passion for writing this book. I know at this stage of this book, you believe me too.

What we need do is what I have stated already. Let me put things in more practical terms for you. Do you see that small street kid just by your house? Do you know you can change our entire nation, your city and the life of that child if you will send him to school and expose him to opportunities?

Do you know that if you will be inspired by what you have read in this book and you will choose to provide evidence at the legislature of our country or state, you can influence how money is allocated to building human capacity?

Do you know that you can see to the effective implementation of allocation for schools and education?

Do you know that you can volunteer to teach a kid, some kids or a group of kids at a school? Do you know that you can personally mentor a child today? Whatever it is that you have to do in order to bring out the best in somebody else, do it. Whatever it is that you have to do in order to bring about the transformation of our country by developing the potential within yourself and others, then do it.

Do you know you can raise national champions and heroes?

Many exceptional people and people who have rewritten the history of the world were raised in foster care. They were raised by people who chose to believe in the potential they carried, they were modeled by people who chose to believe that every child is a star and must not be allowed to waste.

The Nigerian who makes Drones for the United States Army

In the introductory part of this book, I shared briefly the story of Dr. Osatohanmwen Osemwengie. This is a genius of a Nigerian with no mean feats.

Dr. Osatohanmwen Osemwengie, who comes from Benin, Edo state, joins the list of Nigerians making a difference around the world.

Here's what you should know about Dr. Osato Osemwengie:

1. **He is a successful academic.**

Dr. Osemwengie has four graduate degrees, a Doctorate degree in curriculum and instruction from the University of Cincinnati. He is currently working on his 5th and 6th Master's degree in software engineering at Regis University and Information Systems at the Keller Graduate School of Management.

2. **He is the founder of a US-based University.**

Dr. Osato Osemwengie is the founder of the Open Robotics University; a tuition free engineering degree-granting university that allows people to further exercise their talents and expand their knowledge into all fields related to engineering.

3. **His skill sets him apart from other educational administrators.**

Dr. Osemwengie was selected in 2008 to present at the world robotics championships, having expertly coached robotics and served as software engineering mentor to robotics teams.

4. **He has been recognized both at home and abroad.**

Prior to his trip to the United States in 1982, Dr. Osemwengie served as an administrator of the College of Education, Benin City and was recognized as their Educator of the Year for securing funding used to design and implement pre-service teacher education programs.

He served as the Administrator of the Columbus City School System from 1992 to 2011, where he coordinated staff and student recruitment. He also developed programs to increase staff and student retention. He also taught for five years (1987- 1992) in the aforementioned school district. Dr. Osemwengie was a facilitator for the Bill and Melinda Gates Foundation- sponsored Ohio Leadership for Integrating Technology Initiative (OLIT).

It is true that the science is fast becoming an integral component in the battle of influences all over the world. Even Nigeria is adopting the drone war approach against terrorists currently. This definitely means the country needs great minds like Dr. Osato Osemwengie to help build and develop new technology.

There is no doubt that there is no small statured Nigerian. Given the right chance and opportunities, Nigerians will not only control the world but also make Nigeria the greatest country in the world.

For this to happen however, every Nigerian, you and I must see this vision, we must key into this dream and with determination ensure that it becomes a reality within our lifetime.

What Everyone Needs

Like I said earlier, everyone is only begging for an opportunity. Everyone is only looking for a chance to prove himself. Same way I got a chance to prove myself, everyone is only looking for same opportunity like I got.

I plead with you to provide an opportunity for someone today. What can you do? What can you give to help a child find his voice or opportunity in life? What can you do to take a child off the street?

I will provide more strategies in subsequent chapters.

NUGGETS

- Nothing, absolutely nothing is wrong with Nigeria. What Nigeria is going through currently is a phase in her national life.
- With exceptional young men like Harold Ekeh, I can boast that Nigeria can again become one of the greatest countries in the world.
- Nigerians when given the right soil and nutrition and environment, will grow to become the largest cedar in the forest.
- I dream of that day when Nigeria will have an educational environment like the United States currently has, then we will unleash on the world millions of Champions
- If we all can focus our energy on just creating a better environment for our young people alone, Nigeria will become the greatest country in the world.
- American kids themselves do not have admission into their own schools, the 8 Ivy League schools. A feat which is almost synonymous to Nigerian and symbolic of There is a future in every child, there is a genius in every Nigerian kid just waiting for the right environment to manifest it. Every Nigerian kid just wants an opportunity.
- Nigeria can become that country with the highest number of Nobel Prize winners in the world.

CHAPTER THREE

MAKING NIGERIA THE GREATEST COUNTRY IN THE WORLD

At this stage of the book, if you are a Nigerian reading this, I know you must be overly excited, because you belong to a very rare race on earth. In fact, you are simply privileged to be a Nigerian. You belong to a set of people that are very peculiar, and your nation has the potential to become one of the strongest nations on earth.

Now gradually you are bringing your mind to that point where you know that it is not impossible for Nigeria to overtake America and all the great nations of the world at the moment. America is indeed a great nation at the moment, no doubt about it. But greater than America is a budding nation called Nigeria? Is my statement that of mere sentiments? Well, let us consider this fact.

The greatness of America, the Greatness of Nigeria

America today, is a melting pot where all nations and tribes under the sun collate. Hardly can you find a better platform to access practically every nation on earth. But do you also know this surprising fact about America?

Friends, listen to this: NIGERIAN IMMIGRANTS HAVE THE HIGHEST LEVEL OF EDUCATION IN HOUSTON AND IN THE UNITED STATES OF AMERICA IN GENERAL, surpassing whites and Asians, according to a Census data bolstered by an analysis of 13 annual Houston-area surveys, the Houston Chronicle reports. According to a 2006 American Community Survey conducted by the U.S. Census Bureau, 17 percent of all Nigerians in the US hold a Master's degree, 4 percent hold a doctorate and 37 percent have a bachelor's degree.

In comparison, 8% of the white population in the U.S. hold a Master's degree, 1% hold a doctorate and 19% have a bachelor's degree.

Could this also be prove of my earlier statement that America is the Setting sun and Nigeria is the rising sun?

Nigerian-Americans have long been known for their community's intense cultural emphasis on education, and then, there is the analysis of Census data coupled with several local surveys which shows that Nigerians don't just value education, but surpass all other U.S. ethnic groups when it comes to obtaining degrees.

"Being Black, you are already at a disadvantage", Oluyinka Olutoye, an associate professor of pediatric surgery at Baylor College of Medicine, told the Houston Chronicle. "You really need to excel far above if you want to be considered for anything in this country."

David Olowokere, originally from Nigeria and the chairman of Texas Southern University's department of engineering technologies, told a news agency that holding a master's degree just wasn't good enough for his people back home. So he got a doctorate. His wife, Shalewa Olowokere is a civil engineer and hold a master's degree.

However, Stephen Klineberg, a Sociologist at Rice University who conducts the annual Houston Area Survey, suspects the percentage of Nigerian immigrants with post-graduate degrees is higher than the Census data shows.

According to the latest Census data there are more than 12,000 Nigerians in Houston. This is a figure sociologists and Nigerian community leaders say is a gross undercount, as they believe the number is closer to 100,000.

Out of all the Nigerian immigrants Kleinberg reached in his random phone surveys in 1994 through 2007 - a total of 45 households - 40 percent of them told him they had post-graduate degrees.

The reasons Nigerians have more post-graduate degrees than any other racial or ethnic group is largely due to the Nigerian society's emphasis on mandatory and free education, another news agency reports. After immigrating to the U.S., practical matters of immigrations laws get in the way. The Immigration and Nationality Act of 1965 made it easier for Africans to enter the U.S., but mostly as students or highly skilled professionals - not through family sponsorships, Kleinberg said.

What does this imply? If Nigerians can be the best on foreign soil, if Nigeria can make these bold statements in foreign America, then there is nothing stopping her from becoming the greatest country in the world.

Let's face it, the education facilities in Nigerian schools, from Primary School to University level are inferior to that of the US. Also, the level of preparations in Nigerian universities is relatively low. Students are trained to know what is in the book. The practical area is weak, but in spite of all that, when a Nigerian leaves our substandard schools to a very competitive school environment like America they still beat the rest of the world to it.

For all these Nigerians to excel in a very competitive society and environment like America, it goes a long way to point out the potential of our people.

This is same potential that rests within every Nigerian being in Nigeria. This means with a little improvement of our educational system, soon enough, Nigerians can be the most educated nation in the world.

It is true that the reality on ground is challenging. More than 50 percent of our people are not educated. This is a crisis we've got on our hands. But also, when we consider the potential of our people and the things we can achieve, then we will know that we need urgent reforms in the educational sector.

Nigerians are Scaling a Wall

The challenges of modern education is making education personal for each person and increasing everyone's access to knowledge. This is a key area where Nigeria must lead the world and teach the world. We must show the world that education can be personal and every citizen can be educated. When we work actively with this program, Nigeria will become the most educated country in the world within the space of about ten years. There is no doubt about it that Nigeria is the rising sun and America is the setting sun. Even an American, Professor Amy Chua readily agrees that America is on a fast decline.

Professor Amy Chua is of the Yale law school. She and her husband Jed Rubenfeld (a fellow Yale law professor) have written what may turn out to be one of the most honest books of recent times.

It is titled "The Triple Package" because it argues that three qualities are found in spectacularly successful groups in America. These three qualities, they say, are a superiority complex, insecurity and impulse control.

In the book, they shot down many of the popular beliefs about upward mobility in America and about the kinds of people who succeed.

At a time when so many in academia and the media are proclaiming that the poor are no longer able to rise in America, Amy Chua and Jed Rubenfeld point out that a major research project on which that conclusion has been based left out immigrants including Nigerians.

In their own words, *"Although rarely mentioned in media reports, the studies said to show the demise of upward mobility in America largely exclude immigrants and their children. Indeed, the Pew Foundation study most often cited as proof of the death of upward mobility in the United States expressly cautions that its findings do not apply to 'immigrant families,' for whom 'the American dream is alive and well.'"* Nigerians are thriving even more than Americans in America.

Some immigrant groups have risen spectacularly, even when they arrived here with very little money and sometimes with little knowledge of English. *"Almost 25 percent of Nigerian households make over $100,000 a* *year"* in America, the authors point out, compared to just 11 percent of black American households.

Despite many who argue that black Americans cannot rise because of racist barriers, black immigrants rise. A majority of the black students at Harvard are from Africa or the Caribbean, and Nigerians *"are already markedly overrepresented at Wall Street investment banks and blue-chip law firms"*, the two professors claimed in their book.

Amy Chua and Jed Rubenfeld wrote about America. But similar patterns can be found in England, where the white underclass seems to be stuck at the bottom, while low-income non-white immigrant children outperform them in the schools, just as Asian immigrant children outperform white underclass children in America.

This is the power of Nigerians, this is the force of Nigeria. Confidently, I am making the claim that Nigeria will one day lead the world and become the greatest country in the world.

If the immigrants in America will lead Americans in their own country, how much more will they achieve if they were in their own homeland. When Nigerians have conducive conditions like they do in the US, then we will not just have thousands of Nigerians teaching Americans, we will have millions of intelligent and exceptional Nigerians beaming their lights for the world to see.

Nigeria is indeed an exceptional country, one of the rarest countries on earth.

Exceptional Feats by Nigerians

3 Nigerians from same family made history in American university

THEY are biological siblings from same parents in Nigeria. They are Nigerians from Otun local government area of Ekiti State. By dint of hardwork, they prove to the world that Ekiti state is indeed the fountain of knowledge in Nigeria.

Unassuming Seni Ajibade, Tola Ajibade and Femi Ajibade were full of smiles as their various midnight-oil, sleepless nights and sacrifice to become the best in America paid off, as their academic excellence and their GP were best in the entire set of graduating students.

The Ajibades were given a standing ovation for their academic brilliance, godly-virtues, calm demeanor and exceptional attitude by the lecturers and students as well.

All the way in Mercer University, Georgia, United States, the Ajibades have become heroes to African-Americans, Americans and Latino community. They have become inspiration to other students in Mercer University, and other neighbouring varsities. Seni, Tola and Femi have carried the torch of excellence to become one of the latest graduates of medicine at Mercer University, Georgia, USA.

For the records, Seni and Femi are twins, and Tola is their younger sister. The three of them distinguished themselves as outstanding students over the years starting from their days as secondary school students in Nigeria.

When 50% of Graduating PhD Class are Nigerians

It is noteworthy that the Ajibades graduated the same week in May 2016 during commencement of Howard University's 148th Commencement convocation in Washington D.C., 43 out of 96 graduating Doctor of Pharmacy candidates were also Nigerian indigenes with Nigerians taking more than half of the awards at the ceremony.

When in an American University and for a degree as tasking as Pharmacy, and a program highly valued as the PhD, Nigerians form more than 50 percent of the graduating class, what else will be needed to convince the world that this country called Nigeria will not just one day become the greatest country in the world, it probably is one of the greatest countries in the world right now.

Now dear reader, let us paint a picture for ourselves to behold. Imagine a country where we have all of these esteemed minds and educated folks living within a single geographical space, all using their knowledge to build their fatherland. What would it mean for the fortunes of the country?

Such days are upon us. The glory days are here. Soon, all of these Nigerian minds will be working to develop Nigeria. Nigeria will become the greatest entity in the world. There will be no place like Nigeria. All the citizens of the rest of the world will be jostling over themselves to get the Nigerian visa and Passport. That is what is about to happen to Nigeria.

I challenge the government to prevent the brain drain, where the best among us is working for the rest of the countries but for our own selves. We must find a way to attract all of these brains back to Nigeria. We must create whatever will be needed to have these men and women working within us and for us.

Having a PhD also means that you have contributed meaningfully to a field of knowledge through research. The research programs of all of these Nigerians must be funded to create opportunities for the country. There is no doubt that many of the projects that has been created by these people will go on to become global products that will place Nigeria and her products far ahead of those of other nations. There must be a scheme that readily addresses these urgent need. For lack of better opportunities, many of our scholars have fled Nigeria to other places in the world in search of nurture for their ideas. We must nurture the ideas of our own people and not allow government of other countries to nurture them for us at our own loss.

There is no doubt that if we have these men and women within Nigeria, Nigeria will become the pride of the world within a decade.

Nigeria is not just the greatest in the world when it comes to brains and scholarly prowess, there are a lot more things that set Nigeria apart too. For example, do you know that Nigeria is home to the fourth highest number of languages spoken in the world?

Nigeria's Distinction in the World

Languages

Nigeria, with 521 languages has the fourth most languages in the world. This includes 510 living languages, two second languages without native speakers and 9 extinct languages.

Nigeria is home to seven percent (7%) of the total languages spoken on earth. Taraba state alone has more languages than 30 African countries. The importance of this fact is appreciated when one understands that language is the "soul of culture" (as Ngugi wa Thiongo famously said). It is language that births the proverbs, riddles, stories and other aspects of culture that give us identity. UNESCO puts forward that the world's languages represents an extraordinary wealth of creativity. Linguistic diversity correlates with cultural diversity. This means Nigeria can look inwards and drive itself to become the greatest hub for cultural tourism on earth, and consequently empower its citizens tremendously in the process.

With the enormous potential of our cultural tourism, there is no reason why Nigeria should be dependent on the revenue from oil. Exploring the opportunities that exist in our language, we can build ultramodern language centers, and Nigeria can become the holy land of language for the world.

Nigeria can open up more language degrees and programs in our Universities and advertise them for the world. This will see a lot of foreigners trooping to our campuses, itching to learn everything as it regards to the language and culture of our people. In fact, we can build language Universities that can explore every opportunities that our linguistic diversity presents.

Our language degree programs are an important asset. If we find the courage to adapt the way we deliver them to the multilingual reality of our local community and the global world, then we will be in the best position to counteract divisive attitudes in our society, and to lead on delivering the experience, values, and skills that are desperately needed to ensure equality, community cohesion, and competitiveness.

Our young people can create technologies and Apps that presents and teaches our many languages to the world. This will create enormous job opportunities and income for many people.

This rare opportunity of linguistic diversity is not even available in America despite having a population almost more than twice that of Nigeria.

According to the United States census Bureau, the most comprehensive data ever released on languages in the U.S., at least 350 languages are spoken in American homes. Compare that to 521 languages spoken in Nigeria despite having smaller population size and little amount of immigrants. By the time immigrants begin to flood Nigeria looking for opportunities, I predict that well over a thousand languages may be spoken in Nigeria.

Nigeria is not just home to diverse languages, in fact Nigeria is home to everything diversity

TRIBES

For example, Recent statistics has shown that there is over 500 different tribes in Nigeria, while most people are very much aware of the three major tribes in Nigeria; Hausa Igbo and Yoruba, there myriad of others that are yet in obscurity

Hausa-Fulani is the biggest tribe in Nigeria they are the major inhabitants of about 10 state in Nigeria which includes; Bauchi, Borno, Niger,Taraba, Jigawa, Kaduna, Kano, Kastina, Kebbi, Sokoto with traces in several other parts of the country.

The myth or origin of the Hausas began with the story of a man (Bayajidda) who ran away from the east to escape his fathers fury and stumbled on some people that happened to be the today Hausa.

The people (the Hausas) were Guarded (according to the myth) by a sacred snake that prevented them from getting water from their stream six days in a week. The man who later became their founder met a blacksmith who fashioned a knife with which he killed the snake and freed the people. In appreciation they gave him the princess of the land and they gave birth to the seven sons that made up the seven initial Hausa clans.

The Yorubas are the second amongst other Nigerian tribes, The Yoruba spiritual heritage signifies that the Yoruba tribe are a unique people who had their origin at Ile-Ife.

Yoruba people remain one of the most traveled and advanced people from Western part of Africa.

The Igbos are the third largest tribe in Nigeria, they are the Nigerian industrialists. The Igbo myth of Origin traces thier origin from Nri.

Apart from the Hausa, Igbo and Yorubas, Nigeria is home to more than 500 different tribes, again one of the largest of such seen anywhere in the world.

Apart from the above mentioned three major tribes in Nigeria, there are about five hundred-plus other tribes like the Amo, Anaguta, Andoni, Angas, dupe, Ibibio, Idoma, Ikwerre, Kalabari, Abou, Ijaw and several others.

With such people of different backgrounds dwelling together, there is no doubt that existing in unity and as a nation has been very challenging, especially as reflected in the very destructive civil war the nation went through. But then, a good student of the Nigerian history knows that the civil war was a major deviation from the Unity, tolerance and acceptance that Nigeria stood for. So many facts before and after independence, before the civil war stands to this fact and attests to this truth. What do I mean?

In 1956 the first Mayor in a place called Enugu, among the Igbos was a Fulani man by the name of Mallam Umaru Altine. He was not appointed but elected TWICE as Mayor.

Also, the people of Port Harcourt elected a man called Chief John Umolu (from Etsako in today's Edo State, Western region at that time) to represent its municipality in the Eastern Region House of Assembly.

In 1959 the Eastern House of Chiefs was constituted and a man named Mallam Umaru Yushau, the Sarkin Hausawa or Chief of the Hausas in Onitsha, was elected a member of the Eastern House of Chiefs.

In 1957 in a city called Kano, in the heart of Northern Nigeria, one Felix Okonkwo, an Ibo was elected as a special member of the Northern House of Chiefs.

In 1950 in Lagos Nigeria, Olorunimbe was the first Mayor of Lagos with Mazi Mboni Ojike, another Ibo as his deputy

In 1952 a man from Ogwashi Ukwu, in the heart of Igboland by the name of Chike Ekwuiyasi represented Benin West in the Western House of Assembly.

In 1961, the people of Aba voted Margret Ekpo to represent them and Abakaliki voted Chief Eyo Bassey both non-Igbos into parliament.

Alhaji Ibrahim Abubakar Imam from Maiduguri represented Tivland Gboko in the House of Representatives.

Before all these, an astute politician and leader of the Yorubas at the time, Obafemi Awolowo led the campaign for Ernest Ikoli, an Ijaw man who defeated Chief Akinsanya in an election in Lagos. Nnamdi Azikiwe, the leader of the Ibo people led the NCNC his political party to a clean sweep of legislative seats in Lagos which was in the heart of Yoruba land.

A Ghanaian Barrister practicing in Calabar called Atta Munu represented his town of residence in the first legislature in this country elected by universal adult suffrage.

This must seem really exciting to the young people who have always imagined that Nigeria has always been a place where tribalism and nepotism reigns, this was the way it really was and the way we were. This is the way it should be and what we must return to.

Nigeria is not a divided nation and can never be a divided nation. In fact, the rest of the world continues to look on in awe as a nation that has been predicted to break up has defied all negative prophecies and continues to wax stronger despite numerous challenges.

After the amalgamation of the different groups and tribes in 1914 by Lord Lugard, many people only saw everything wrong with the amalgamation and predicted that the nation will not be able to exist. In fact, certain historians predicted that the amalgamation would be short-lived and will not last up to fifty years, well the amalgamation of Nigeria is well over hundred years old and still counting.

What this means is that we are a people of common destiny. We will always overcome all odds and teach the rest of the world how to dwell together in unity.

Nigeria's Strength Despite Challenges

Considering events and happenings around the world, many nations of the world not as diverse as Nigeria have gone up in tubes and many broke in war due to consistent misunderstanding and fighting. In the midst of all her problems however, Nigeria continues to dwell together in peace and harmony, showcasing the beauty in diversity to the world.

Merit, character and patriotism used to hold sway and the country kept pace with the world. When we failed in this values as a country, we began to misunderstand ourselves. A deviation from values is the reason why nations fail. I have developed and discussed every point on this topic in another book called, **WHY COUNTRIES FAIL**. However, with the power of values which is inherent in us, we will rebuild our nation again. We will make Nigeria the greatest country in the world.

Earlier I said that Nigeria is home to everything diversity. Even the birds of the air prove it.

BIRDS

A good example of this is the Jos Plateau Indigo bird, a small reddish-brown bird, which is found nowhere else on the planet but Plateau state, Nigeria.

Also, the Anambra waxbill, a small bird of many beautiful colors, is found only in Southern Nigeria and nowhere else on earth. These are only small proportions of the peculiarity of this individual entity called Nigeria.

I think peculiarities such as this should be the focus of our government. Since we are a people of easy distinction, we must be looking for how to turn all of our distinctions into wealth.

The Niger Delta which is the second largest delta on earth is in Nigeria. It has the highest concentration of monotypic fish families in the world, and is also home to sixty percent of Nigeria's mangrove forests. You should know too that Nigeria's mangrove forests are the largest in Africa and third largest on earth.

With such enormous forest reserve, the possibilities of wealth creation is endless. Lack of Jobs should be a very foreign word in Nigeria.

Also according to the World Resources Institute, Nigeria is home to 4,715 different types of plant species, and over 550 species of breeding birds and mammals, making it one of the most ecologically vibrant places of the planet. This of course is a major reason the world should look up to Nigeria.

In addition, areas surrounding Cross River State and Calabar towards the south of Nigeria are home to the largest diversity of butterflies in the world.

Many people do not know that the rarest species of animals are found in Nigeria. In fact, two of the world's rarest species of animals live in the mysterious Nigerian forests - the Drill monkey that lives in the Afi Mountain ranges and the lowland Gorilla. What a beauty, what a distinction. You must begin to understand why I said it is a great privilege to be born a Nigerian.

In fact, there are about 49 animals found nowhere else on the planet except in Nigeria. Mammals found nowhere else in the world include Sclater's Guenon, Fox's Shaggy Rat, the Gotel Mountains Soft-furred Mouse, the Savanna Swamp Shrew , and a recently described forest shrew Sylvisorex corbeti .

The Ibadan Malimbe is a bird unique to only Nigeria on the surface of the earth.

Among about 80 vascular plant species exclusive to Nigeria are the orchids Genyorchis apertiflora, Genyorchis summerhayesiana, Habenaria linguiformis and Diaphananthe dorotheae. Other endemic plants include Costus talbotii.

At this stage of the book, I want to challenge the Nigerian government to set up a whole commission that can effectively manage this rarest species found nowhere else in the world but Nigeria. We must protect all of these animals and plants from extinction. There is a reason they are given exclusively to Nigeria by God and it further announces our uniqueness to the world. It shows that Nigeria is the natural leader of the emerging world.

IGBO ORA: THE TWINS' CAPITAL OF THE WORLD

Among the rarity that is found in Nigeria is a town called Igbo Ora the twin capital of the world. This means in the entire planet, this small city of Nigeria has the highest rate of twin births in the world.

Igbo Ora is one town in Oyo State Nigeria situated north of Lagos. The town is the headquarters of Ibarapa Central Local Government Area of Oyo State. It is situated between Sagaun, Iberekedo, Idofin and Abeokuta. This farming community which has seen little development in spite of its popularity is known for two things!

First, it is known in Oyo state as the 6th largest charcoal producing town.

Then, it is known internationally as The Twins-Capital of the World.

Yes, you read it correctly. In fact, a signage at the entrance to the town affirms this claim. And to cap it up, every family there has a set of twins.

Statistics from various sources have indicated that there are about 158 twins per 1000 births in Igbo Ora. To back up this claim, a British gynecologist Patrick Nylander carried out a research in the 80's and the results showed that there are about 45-50 twins per 1000 births. Most people believe the statistics may have doubled by now.

So what's so special about the Igbo Ora people that made them this fertile? What is the reason for the high rate of twins in Igbo Ora, Oyo state, Nigeria?

This is one unanswered question that has been on the lip of many people as there has been not enough scientific research to determine the real reason behind the twinning rate of the Igbo Ora people. Most people have their own views about the matter.

According to an article on Neoblack, the Olu of Igbo Ora Oba Oyewale Oyerogba in an interview in 2013 said *"we eat a lot of okro leaf or ilasa soup. We also consume a lot of agida (yam). These diets influence multiple births."* This is the same view many of the Igbo Ora people believe in. In another oral interview with a woman from the town, she revealed that she was a twin, she had twins who also had twins. Even her twin had twins that also had twins.

But she isn't the only woman like that in Igbo Ora. As a matter of fact, the women that sell the "leaf" used for making the soup are called Iya Ibeji (mother of twins).

Even though there has been no scientific evidence for the high birth rate of twins, experts believe that the reason for the high twinning rate is embedded in their genes as they descended from ancestors to ancestors. They opined that their ancestors must have eaten a lot of yams which contains certain elements that increases a woman's chances of fertilization. But these claims have been rendered useless by the mere fact that neighboring communities who eat the yam and also make the soup haven't been as successful as Igbo Ora when it comes to twins.

This very special feature has made Igbo Ora a tourist city and a center for fertility research. Many researchers simply troop to this small town of Igbo Ora in search for fertility and multiple birth solutions for women.

Do not be surprised if the cure to infertility all over the world is found in this small city of Nigeria. Nigeria was designed for such feats, especially as the soon-to-be-greatest country in the world.

Finally in this chapter, permit me to share with you the unique story of Nigeria's Mrs Esther Taiwo Olukoya and Mrs Emily Kehinde Olukoga-Ogunde, who looked almost identical, and are probably the third set of twins in the world to hit the century age and perhaps the first in Africa.

Nigerians too want to live long. The life expectancy rate among our citizens should not just be another topic of debate anymore but strategies should be developed to help Nigerians live longer. If this set of twins could live such long lives, then it is not impossible for majority of our citizens within Nigeria. It must not be that until our citizens leave the shores of the country before their quality of lives improve.

This chapter has dealt with the uniqueness of Nigeria so far and why Nigeria could the leader of the new world. Everything to make Nigeria the greatest nation in the world already rests within her.

We have looked at attributes of Nigeria that makes her an example to the rest of the world. Attributes such as Religious tolerance: Religious tolerance, though a bit hard to preach this in the light of recent Boko Haram terror but generally Nigeria is multi-religious and handling it well in most cases especially in the western and eastern Nigeria.

We allow everyone worship as long as they do not threaten the civil liberties of others. Also resilience and flexibility is a strong Nigerian trait: Nigerian culture is fixed in some ways but very flexible in others. In spite of the pressures of modern culture or globalization, some of our cultural habits have proven very resilient. New religions, languages, food, musical instruments have been embraced and adopted and the old substitutes have been moved around and either improved or given new roles without diminishing them (This does not negate the need to do more work to preserve our uniqueness). With over 500 ethnic groups dwelling together…Though there has been speculations about break up, that is not going to happen.

There is no doubt that joining hands, Nigerians can make Nigeria the greatest country on the planet.

NUGGETS

- Exploring the opportunities that exist in our language, we can build ultramodern language centers, and Nigeria can become the holy land of language for the world.
- Nigeria is not a divided nation and can never be a divided nation.
- Since Nigerians are a people of easy distinction, we must be looking for how to turn all of our distinctions into wealth.
- Nigeria is the natural leader of the emerging world.
- Do not be surprised if the cure to infertility all over the world is found in the small city of Igbo Ora Nigeria.
- Resilience and flexibility is a strong Nigerian trait: Nigerian culture is fixed in some ways but very flexible in others.
- There has been speculations about break up of Nigeria, which is not going to happen.
- There is no doubt that joining hands, Nigerians can make Nigeria the greatest country on the planet.

CHAPTER FOUR

SIGNIFICANT CONTRIBUTIONS OF NIGERIANS TO THE WORLD

Earlier, I put it to you that the Jews are one of the strongest nations in the world right now. I also made a claim that what the Jews have achieved is nothing compared to what Nigerians can do if we set our mind to it. I told you how Jews have caused a monumental revolution in the world just by accepting who they are. I am now explaining to you how we too as Nigerians can bring about a shocking and rapid development, the type that the world has never experienced before, not just to our country and continent but to the world.

This is very possible, it is what the Jews have succeeded in doing.

In a previous chapter, we saw briefly the extent of impact of Jews on the world using different markers. The Nobel Prize is a category in which Jews have largely excelled. I am going to discuss this in greater details in later pages.

In this chapter, I am putting forward Nigerians who are not anyway less than Nobel Prize winners. In fact, I foresee many of this Nigerians winning the Nobel Prize if they are further encouraged in their endeavors. One of such people is a man who has been described as Nigeria's golden boy, Phillip Emeagwali.

DR. PHILIP EMEAGWALI - NIGERIA'S GOLDEN CHILD

Emeagwali was born August 23, 1954 in Akure, a remote city in Nigeria. He was the oldest of nine children and was considered a child prodigy because he was an excellent math student. His father spent lots of time helping and nurturing Emeagwali with mathematics. He was so good in math that by the time he got to high school, he was performing so well that his classmates nicknamed him "**Calculus**".

A couple years after, he dropped out of school because a civil war broke out and he was drafted into the Biafran army. That did not deter Emeagwali, and when the war ended, he continued to study at the local public library. There, in the library, he taught himself advanced math, physics, and chemistry by studying on his own, and at the age of 17, completed his high school equivalence test and won a scholarship to study mathematics at Oregon State University.

He obtained a BS in mathematics. He also earned three other degrees - a PhD in scientific computing from the University of Michigan and two Masters degrees from George Washington University.

Dr. Philip Emeagwali also received acclaim, at least in part, on his study of nature, specifically bees. Emeagwali saw an inherent efficiency in the way bees construct and work with honeycomb and determined computers that emulate this process would be the more efficient and more powerful. In the year 1989, emulating the bees' honeycomb construction, Emeagwali used 65,000 processors to invent the world's fastest computer, which performs computations at 3.1 billion calculations per second.

Dr. Philip Emeagwali's resume is loaded with many other such feats, including ways of making oil fields more productive - which has resulted in the United States saving hundreds of millions of dollars each year. As one of the most famous African-American inventors of the 20th century, Dr. Emeagwali also has won the Gordon Bell Prize - the Nobel Prize for computation. His computers are currently being used to forecast the weather and to predict the likelihood and effects of future global warming.

Emeagwali wanted to become a mathematician, physicist or astronomer. He could not study these subjects at the cutting-edge level in Africa, so he went to the United States. During the week that he arrived in the United States, he went to an airport, used a telephone, used a library, talked with a scientist, and was shown a computer for the first time in his life.

In 1989 he won the Gordon Bell Prize. He accessed the Connection Machine over the Internet. The Connection Machines owned by the United States government laboratories were made available to him because they were considered impossible to program and there was no great demand for them at that time. In fact, the national laboratories that purchased them were embarrassed because their scientists could not program them and they were hardly being used. The labs were happy that Emeagwali was brave enough to attempt to program it and the million computer was left entirely to his use. He was, in a sense, their human guinea pig.

Today, he has access to a million super computer while many African scientists do not have access to any personal computer. The greater opportunity enabled him to make important discoveries and inventions.

The Connection Machine was the most powerful supercomputer in the world. It is a complex supercomputer, briefly, to program it requires an absolute understanding of how all 65,536 processors are interconnected. The processing nodes are configured as a cube in a 12-dimensional universe, although we only use it to solve problems arising from our three-dimensional universe.

To perform the world's fastest computation, he divided and evenly distributed the calculations among the 65,536 processors and then squeezed the most performance from the each processor. It took him 1057 pages to describe the hundreds of mathematical equations, algorithms and programming techniques that he invented and used. The details would be of interest to mathematicians and super computer nerds only. This discovery helps analyze petroleum fields and does massive calculations.

Like I earlier said, Dr. Philip Emeagwali's resume is loaded with many other such feats, including ways of making oil fields more productive – which has resulted in the United States saving hundreds of millions of dollars each year. His computers are currently being used to forecast the weather and to predict the likelihood and effects of future global warming.

I have no doubt in my heart that given the same opportunity as Dr. Emeagwali, there are many more Nigerians that would perform as well if not better. Our land abounds with millions of Emeagwalis. Nigeria surely can teach the world.

With all these human tools who are yet alive that Nigeria can pool from, there is no excuse for Nigeria to still be a third world country today. That is an insult on everything that we stand for.

What is more amusing is that the nations of the world are filled with many more Nigerians like Dr Phillip Emeagwali, many more examples which I will share with you in this chapter. There is therefore no reason under the sun why a nation like Nigeria should suffer while we have men of such caliber being used by other countries to develop their own states.

For a man like Phillip Emeagwali and men like him, they need to be invited by the Nigerian senate and government to come invest in Nigeria. In fact, they need to become the investment of the Nigerian Government. Phillip and colleagues need to put similar structures in our educational curriculum. He needs to be given lands to build computer villages and reproduce himself in Nigeria. There is no stopping us now. Nigeria can raise and must be challenged to raise a million other Phillip Emeagwalis.

First Doctor to Birth a Baby Twice in the World is a Nigerian

In 2017, a ground breaking surgery happened in the United States when for the first time a baby was born twice. Guess who was responsible for this extra ordinary feat? Dr. Oluyinka Olutoye, a Nigerian doctor and another Dr Cass of the United States.

The baby had to be 'born twice' after doctors had to take her out of the womb to remove a tumor that was threatening her life.

Lynlee Boemer's only chance of survival was a risky fetal surgery which involved cutting her out of her mother prematurely, and then putting her back in so that she could be carried full term.

Lynlee's mother Margaret said she was told at 16 weeks that her baby was suffering from a rare birth defect known as sacrococcygeal teratoma - a tumor that grows from a baby's tail-bone.

The growth occurs in about one out of 30,000-70,000 live births and affects girls four times more than boys.

In some cases the baby can be left to develop normally in the womb and when it is born doctors can remove the tumor, but in the case of Lynlee, the tumor had begun to take over her blood supply and was putting her heart under immense strain.

Dr Oluyinka Olutoye, offered Mrs Boemer a termination but she wanted to give Lynlee a chance at life so they took the decision to operate on the baby before it was born.

When Mrs Boemer was 23 weeks and five days pregnant she was taken into the operating theatre.

Mrs Boemer told CNN: "Lynlee didn't have much of a chance. At 23 weeks, the tumor was shutting her heart down and causing her to go into cardiac failure, so it was a choice of allowing the tumor to take over her body or giving her a chance at life.

"It was an easy decision for us. We wanted to give her life."

The two surgeons performed the delicate five-hour surgery on the 1lb 3oz fetus by temporarily removing her from the womb.

Dr Cass said the tumor was so large that a huge cut was needed to get the baby out of the uterus.

He added: *"So it ended up that the baby was hanging out in the air... Essentially, the fetus is outside, like completely out, all the amniotic fluid falls out, it's actually fairly dramatic."*

During the surgery Lynlee's heart almost came to a standstill, but Dr Cass credited the heart specialist in the theatre with keeping her alive.

After they had removed as much of the tumour as possible, the surgeons put Lynlee back into the womb and sewed her back into her mother.

Mrs Boemer was then put on bed rest and eventually managed to carry Lynlee to full term before she was 'born again' by cesarean section in June 2017.

However, the ordeal wasn't quite over yet as at eight days old Lynlee had to undergo further surgery to remove remnants of the tumor that could not initially be reached.

Several weeks after her last operation and Lynlee made a remarkable recovery with her family at home. That was the first time such a surgery was being performed in the history of the world.

Olutoye, who obtained his medical degree from the Obafemi Awolowo University, Ile-Ife, Nigeria, in 1988 before his doctoral degree in anatomy from Virginia Commonwealth University in Richmond, VA, in 1996, had relocated from Nigeria to the US to seek further educational opportunities.

He said: *"At the completion of my medical education in Nigeria, I realised that I read about a lot of different aspects of medicine that I didn't have the opportunity to be exposed to locally. I therefore sought further educational opportunities in the United States."*

The Ido Ani, Ondo State-born surgeon is a son of Major-General Olufemi Olutoye (rtd) and Prof. Omotayo Olutoye. He described his childhood as wonderful.

He said: *"I had a wonderful childhood. I was born in Lagos and grew up with two loving parents, (Major-General (rtd) Olufemi Olutoye, OFR and Prof. Omotayo Olutoye); three sisters (Dr. Bunmi Okanlami, Funke Olugboji, 'Toye Gansallo) and two brothers (Air Commodore (rtd) Dr. Femi Olutoye, Dr. Segun Olutoye); grandparents, numerous cousins, uncles and aunties.*

It was, and still is, a wonderful loving environment. We were all taught the importance of hard work and a solid education, and most importantly, the fear of The Lord.

As a son of a soldier father and an academic mother, Olutoye said he was introduced early in life to a life that placed emphasis on the need to strive for excellence. He maintained that the character his parents helped him to inculcate as a child has endured till now.

He said: "*The quest for excellence was introduced at an early age. I attended elementary school at Lagos University Staff School and subsequently King's College Lagos. The character and friendships established in those formative years have endured to date.*

I proceeded to Obafemi Awolowo University, Ile-Ife for my medical education at the Faculty of Health Sciences. There I met my beautiful bride (Prof. 'Toyin Olutoye, nee Balogun) who is an anesthesiologist. We are blessed with two children. I had further training at the Lagos University Teaching Hospital, Idi-Araba, prior to seeking additional training in the USA.

In the USA, I started my post-graduate medical education in pediatrics at Howard University and District of Columbia General Hospital. I then had my general surgery training at Virginia Commonwealth University Hospitals, Richmond Virginia, during which I took time off for research and obtained a Ph.D in Anatomy from Virginia Commonwealth University.

Following my training as a general surgeon, I sought additional training in pediatric, fetal and thoracic surgery at the Children's Hospital of Philadelphia. I then took up a faculty position at Baylor College of Medicine and, with my colleague, Dr. Darrell Cass, established the Texas Children's Fetal Center at Texas Children's Hospital in Houston Texas."

Growing up in such a family, the surgeon said he never wanted to be anything else but a medical doctor. "*I always wanted to be a medical doctor,*" he said in response to what his childhood dream was.

Despite the deluge of negative stories about Nigerians back home, Olutoye and many other Nigerians in the

Diaspora have continued to do great exploits in their host countries. According to Olutoye, such feats are possible when they have access to resources and infrastructure.

"Nigerians are a talented people. If they decide to apply themselves, they can achieve much. When they then have access to resources and infrastructure, they can attain even greater heights," he said.

In the face of growing desperation by young Nigerians who risk their lives to cross the Mediterranean just to get to Europe and America, Olutoye urged Nigerian youths to always note that the grass is not always greener on the other side of the divide.

"Do the best you can with what you have where you are. To quote Eleanor Roosevelt, the grass is not always greener on the other side. Look before you leap," he said.

Given the global attention the feat may have attracted to Olutoye and his colleagues at the Texas hospital, one may want to believe that the people behind the feat would now walk around town with shoulders raised. For Olutoye, however, *"such glory should be given to God."*

Dr Olutoye is just another Nigerian making extra ordinary feats for Nigeria outside the shores of Nigeria. Nigeria cannot but be very proud of these illustrious sons and daughters. There is no doubt that these fine men and women must be attracted back by all means into the shores of Nigeria. These men must become the foundations upon which the Federal government can hinge our development. There is no doubt about it.

Hope for Nigeria

Stories of the likes of Dr Olutoye that I read about every year fills me with enormous hope for Nigeria. Can you see what I see now? This is a reason why I described Nigeria as the rising sun and America as the setting sun. Is it not obvious to see? Nigeria has everything it takes to become the greatest country in the world.

Nigeria is not in any way poor. It is just poorly being managed. Our greatest wealth is in our people. This is why we can become the greatest and the wealthiest nation on earth.

After 130 Years, First Black Harvard Law Review Female President is a Nigerian

The Harvard Law Review is the most prestigious legal journal in the world, but the 130-year-old publication had never elected a black woman as its president - until 2017.

That honor has gone to ImeIme Umana, a 24-year-old daughter of Nigerian immigrants who has been voted president by the Law Review's 92 student editors. Twenty-seven years ago, a Harvard Law School student named Barack Obama was elected the publication's first black male president.

Umana is *"a brilliant, high-energy young woman with a keen sense of social justice and commitment to service"*, said Lawrence D. Bobo, chairman of the Department of African and African-American Studies at Harvard, where Umana earned honors as an undergraduate for her thesis on the adverse effects of voter-identification laws on minority voters.

The Law Review post is considered a key to some of the most coveted doors in the legal profession, but Umana has said she wants to pursue a position as a public defender. The second-year law student was exposed to that work in 2016 during a stint in the public defender's office in the Bronx, N.Y.

Her empathy for the marginalized is well known, professors and classmates said. When she graduated from Harvard College in 2014, Umana received the Rev. Peter J. Gomes Prize, which the African and African-American studies department bestows on the student *"who best epitomizes social responsibility through public service and potential for distinguished contributions to the public good"*, Bobo said.

"Barriers of race and of gender and the places where they intersect continue to crumble, and rightfully so", he said. *"ImeIme Umana is paving a way for future generations of African-American women - indeed, all women of color - as leaders, not just rank and file, in the legal profession of tomorrow."*

Alexa Kissinger, managing editor of the Law Review, praised Umana's election.

"ImeIme has a fierce legal mind, compassion for other members of the team, and unparalleled dedication to this institution", Kissinger said. *"Our class of editors is the most diverse in the history of the Harvard Law Review, and we couldn't be prouder to have ImeIme at the helm"*.

Natalie Vernon, president of the Harvard Women's Law Association, called Umana "universally beloved" on campus.

What more can be said? Another barrier broken and it was by a Nigerian. Nigeria can surely become the greatest country in the world.

If we have such brilliant genes manifested through Umana to the world. There must be several millions of such people on our shores. Hence we must do everything within our power to encourage leadership in our young people. We must give our young Nigerians the platform with which their voice can be heard in the world.

When we are able to provide these platforms for our young people, they will become global players and compete effectively. They will bring ground-breaking solutions to age long problems. Such is the case of the young Nigerian whose story you are about to read.

A Nigerian Scientist Invents Device that can Supply the Entire African Continent Uninterrupted Power Supply

Nigerian engineer, Obayagbona Emmanuel Imafidon, stated in 2017 that he has invented a power-generating device that can solve the power shortage in the country. In an interview with Guardian, the graduate of Electrical Engineering from the Institute of Management and Technology in Enugu said he could generate power from thunder lightning and that he has been working on it since 2006. He said: I have been researching on generating constant power from thunder lightning. That is using a strike of thunder lightning to generate power that can serve Nigeria and Africa for five years and 30 days. That means that whenever thunder strike for once, we are sure of uninterrupted power for five years and thirty days.

One may think it is not possible and if it is possible why the western world has not converted lightning to electricity, but what I have developed so far is a prototype. There are five chambers including the trapping zone which is made of lightning arrestor. There is the storage zone and the conversion zone, which convert static energy into current electricity and transmit the energy into transmission zone. The transmission zones will first of all step down the power from as high as five mega volts and there are five storage zones that have the capacity of storing over 25 mega volts of power. When it stores the 25 MV of power, the conversion zone takes one mega vote at a time, send signals to other sensory zones which shut down other sensory zones from discharging at the same time. Now the transmission zone of the power generating plant will step down the megavolt to whatever Nigerians need. For instance, Nigeria is generating 330,000 megavolts, but my device generate 5 million volts and then give Nigerians their 330 KV and still have about 4670, 000 megavolts left as reserve.

There is a far cry between lightning energy and hydro-electricity which the country relies on. "The trapping zone will be built by the Russians, Germany or USA in order to capture a maximum of 5 mega volts and allow 330,000 megavolts to be wasted in the atmosphere for the trapping arrestor. Now, the five megavolts trapped by lightning will send the signal or energy to the annexing zone. You can see that we have so many trapping zones here and that is because you don't know the direction lightning may come from. So, we cannot use one lightning director to achieve the purpose and that is why we have several lightning arrestors here.

There is no gainsaying the fact that if this young man's research is looked into and validated, he might have brought a permanent solution to the age-long energy problem in Africa. So what is stopping the funding and promoting of such a noble idea.

The young man himself explained it this way, "The Nigerian Stock Exchange (NSE) is there to fund experiments, research, inventions to bring them into limelight. I found out that government set aside funds for research but how the funds are being used is a different kettle of fish. I am emphasizing on NSE because in the USA, when a young person invents anything, all their engineers gather to give their support. But in Nigeria, they will want you to carry out the research alone so that when you fail, they will say you don't know what you are talking about. One major advantages of generating power from lightning is that it will save Nigeria from constant blackout. Every time you hear that water level has dropped and as such we are not able to generate enough electricity. There is no year that thunder does not strike in Nigeria and one strike of lightning can give power for five years and thirty days, then we will have enough power for our home and industrial needs.

The young inventor is simply frustrated that corruption is inhibiting research and discovery in Nigeria today.

Must we allow the rest of our young innovators and scientists suffer brain-drain too? Why does it look like unless Nigerians leave the shores of the country, their ideas are not encouraged? Nations are not built like that.

Immediately we get a flicker of hope anywhere in any of our people, they must be immediately encouraged especially if they are young. We must destroy the impression that our environment only kills potentials, it doesn't support it.

However, it has not been all bad news from Nigeria when it concerns giving support to the young people and their innovative ideas. Some of our innovators have been able to get the support of our government to build their research work in recent times. One of such is the case of Jessica Matthews, the young Nigerian lady who invented the electricity generating football.

When Nigeria Appointed Electricity Generating Football Inventor, Jessica Matthews, as Entrepreneurship Ambassador

In 2013, The Federal Government appointed Jessica Matthews, a U.S.-based Nigerian, who invented energy generating football and skipping rope as an `Entrepreneurship Ambassador'.

The then Minister of Trade and Investments, Dr Olusegun Aganga, announced after the presentation and demonstration of the invented products to the then President Goodluck Jonathan at the Presidential Villa.

Aganga said, *"Mathews is an inspiration to every Nigerian, especially children, and the product is portrayed as made by a Nigerian for the world.*

The product is actually versatile, it is not just about the electricity you see, you can use it to charge your mobile phones and fans so there are so many things for which it can be used.

We are also looking at the possibilities of manufacturing it in Nigeria and see how we can make it cheaper in this country.

I am glad that Matthew has also agreed to be our ambassador in terms of promoting entrepreneurship in our universities.

What we want to do is to bring successful entrepreneurs like Matthew to inspire the students and make them more creative so that they can also be employers of labour," the minister said.

Matthew, an Edo-born inventor, who demonstrated the soccer ball, said it could generate three hours of electricity after 30 minutes of play and could store power for 72 hours.

The electricity generated by the ball, according to her, can be used as electricity source to power lighting points and household equipments.

Mathews, 25, and Co-founder of Uncharted play, said the airless football used as electricity power source when not in use, could span for 18-months before replacement.

The inventor, who studied Psychology and Economics in Havard University, U.S., said she taught herself Electrical and Mechanical Engineering because of her interest in the field

She said her motivation to invent the ball and skipping rope came when she attended a wedding in Nigeria and there was a sudden power outage.

"I am a Nigerian and was in Nigeria, it was my Aunt's wedding and we lost power. How many times, is there anyone who has not been affected?

For me, I was raised to seek a solution when there is a problem. To be as creative as you can and be opened to different ways so you can address the situation", she said.

Mathews, who spoke on why she chose to use football, explained: *"To me, we all know that football is the most popular thing in the world.*

To most people, football form is the most convenient; any man on the street will be attracted to kicking football.

So, the idea is to put something that people really love and get more out of it.

These are the things we can use to see if we can amplify existing behaviour to bridge the gap between what is working and what is not working in this country that we love so much.

We take our passion for sports that is so beautiful and we say okay, let's give people renewable clean power that they can control."

She said the innovation, which had been accepted and already in use in the U.S., would be affordable when mass-produced and introduced into the Nigerian market.

"Right now, if we are going to sell it here in Nigeria, it will be equivalent to what you will pay for a solar inverter.

Right now, we have not started making them here, we are selling them in New York and in New York, we charge people a lot because it is New York", she said.

Dr Reuben Abati, the Special Adviser to the then President on Media and Publicity, said Jonathan congratulated Mathews on her creativity and innovativeness.

"The president is particularly impressed that Matthew is multi-talented, and that she developed herself in science despite that she is a psychologist and economist.

It is a proof of the quality of human resource we have in Nigeria and the president is proud of her", Abati said.

Abati said the president assured that the invention would be used as a major tool to mobilize young children and encourage them to think more deeply.

The Federal government of Nigeria need to be commended for this singular effort, but it is not enough. We need thousands of Matthews to be appointed as ambassadors and sent to our schools, colleges and campuses to inspire the teeming young and creative minds on these campuses. We need trade fairs and exhibitions where young people can showcase talents and creativities.

We need established companies to partner with promising inventions. This can only be achieved through the aid of the government. We need soft loans for young people to encourage them into research and creative works.

When this is done, you can imagine millions of Nigerian youths like Jessica maximizing their potential and bringing out new products every day.

I have shown you thus far in this book that the greatest wealth Nigeria possesses is not the oil wells and the petroleum fields. No, the greatest wealth of Nigeria is raw untapped human resource. I dare say that Nigeria only needs to maximize up to about 40% of her human resource potential and she will be among the greatest nation in the world.

It was indeed a happy news when the Federal Government of Nigeria appointed Jessica Matthews as an ambassador of entrepreneurship in Nigeria. Before her, a reputable Nigerian in the United States, Professor Bart Nnaji too had been invited back to Nigeria and appointed Minister of Power.

Bartholomew Nnaji - Powering Nigeria

A scientist, innovator and one of the inventors of the E-Design concept, he has proven that mankind can only be limited by her imagination. In a fundamental sense, he is the man who saw tomorrow having explored and is still exploring the exciting frontiers of knowledge.

He has put Nigeria on the world map for the right reasons - for a change. Meet Dr. Bartholomew Nnaji, born on 13 July 1956, in Enugu State.

He earned a Bachelor of Science degree in physics at St John's University, and then proceeded to the Virginia Polytechnic Institute and State University for postgraduate studies.

He joined the faculty at University of Massachusetts Amherst in 1983. After a few years, he became the director and a founder of the Automation and Robotics Laboratory at the University. He was made a professor of mechanical and industrial engineering in 1992.

As a researcher, he focused on three major topics: Computer Aided Design, Robotics and Computer Aided Engineering.

Using the knowledge he gained from his research pursuits, he created the term geometric reasoning, the idea that most things we operate has a geometric configuration. He is also credited as one of the innovators of the E-design concept.

Nnaji built upon his previous experience in Nigeria's power sector to create his company, the first indigenous owned power generating company in Nigeria. In 1993, he served as Federal Minister of Science and Technology.

In 2000, along with his joint venture partner Renatech International Limited, Nnaji built and managed a successful 15MW emergency power station in Abuja. In 2003, Nnaji began traveling back and forth to Nigeria to build a world-class, indigenous power company.

He is currently Chairman and CEO of the company, Geometric Power Limited, or GPL, a US$250 million, 140 MW, integrated generation and distribution power plant.

On 28 August 2012, Nnaji resigned as Nigeria's Minister of Power amid unconfirmed reports that he was linked to a company bidding for a lucrative electricity contract.

Nnaji captures his vision for reinventing Nigeria's nightmarish power sector: *"I have a fundamental belief that there is nowhere that it is written 'on the forehead of Nigeria' that 'thou shall not have reliable quality and affordable electricity'.*

Our goal is to build Power projects that make economic sense and at the same time have social value that can lift the quality of life of our customers and the community". From a statement accorded to Dr Nnaji.

This is the blueprint to develop Nigeria. This is the pathway to our growth. Same way Dr Nnaji through all odds was made to serve in Nigeria, this must be achieved with all of our exceptional sons and daughters. There is no doubt that soon enough Nigeria will be riding on the waves of glory. Inventions will be pouring down like torrents of rain. Growth and development will be so rapid like what the world had never seen or experienced before.

Now, I know your conviction is becoming solid on the fact that Nigeria can become the greatest country in the world.

This must become our new song and we must not give ourselves any rest until we achieve this. Only then would we have attained our destiny as a nation, as the largest black country in the world. Are you interested in more facts, evidences and the pathway out of our current gloom, then follow me into the next chapter.

NUGGETS

- Nigeria can raise and must be challenged to raise a million other Phillip Emeagwalis.
- Nigeria is not in any way poor. It is just poorly being managed. Our greatest wealth is in our people.
- We must do everything within our power to encourage leadership in our young people
- When we are able to provide platforms for our young people, they will become global players and compete effectively
- Must we allow the rest of our young innovators and scientists suffer brain-drain too? Why does it look like unless Nigerians leave the shores of the country, their ideas are not encouraged?
- We need established companies to partner with promising inventions.
- The greatest wealth Nigeria possesses is not the oil wells and the petroleum fields. No, the greatest wealth of Nigeria is raw untapped human resource.
- There is no doubt that soon enough Nigeria will be riding on the waves of glory. Inventions will be pouring down like torrents of rain.

CHAPTER FIVE

STEPS TO TRANSFORMING NIGERIA

Having seen the monumental achievements of Nigerians in many universities and institutions of the world, we have shown Nigeria in the light of a leading nation.

In this chapter, it is imperative that we look at the methods and strategies that Nigeria can employ to achieve so much within a little space of time, hence recover her lost years. It is my belief that if Nigeria will go back to the same principles that her excelling sons and daughters are employing outside the boundaries of the country, if these principles will be used to administer our nation, we may not be too far again from glory road.

Among many things that we have observed in these men and women, one of them is pivotal and paramount and it became the major tool for their success. Remember, we established at the initial part of this book that Nigerians are extremely gifted people, capable of solving any problems by themselves. In other words, given the right environment, Nigerians are capable of building anything that needs to be built.

Now, we want to consider how certain Nigerians have practically done the impossible in the world. Many of what Nigerians have achieved is almost unbelievable. Here are a few, read for yourself.

Adebayo Ogunlesi: the Nigerian Wonder

One reason why I believe Nigeria is the rising star of the future is in what the rest of the world would refuse to believe. WHO COULD HAVE BELIEVED THAT A NIGERIAN OWNS THE SECOND LARGEST INTERNATIONAL AIRPORT IN ALL OF GREAT BRITAIN? Here is the story:

Up until February 2010, very few people had heard about Adebayo Ogunlesi. The Nigerian-born investment banker and money manager made international headlines when he led the acquisition of London's Gatwick Airport from the British Airports Authority in a recorded £1.51 billion deal. The acquisition instantly propelled Ogunlesi, 58, into the global spotlight and earned him a place in history as the man who acquired London's second largest international airport.

Adebayo Ogunlesi is the chairman and managing partner of Global Infrastructure Partners (GIP), a New York-based independent private equity fund focused primarily on infrastructural investments, with over $5.6 billion under his management. The purchase of Gatwick Airport may have grabbed all the headlines, but GIP has some other noteworthy assets in its portfolio including a 75% stake in London City Airport, and Biffa Limited, a UK based waste management company.

Adebayo "Bayo" O. Ogunlesi was born December 20, 1953 to the family of Prof. & Mrs. T.O. Ogunlesi of Makun, Sagamu, Ogun State. His father was the first Nigerian professor of Medicine.

Young Ogunlesi obtained his Secondary School education from the prestigious King's College in Lagos.

He received a B.A. with first class honors in Philosophy, Politics and Economics from Oxford University in London, England before proceeding to Harvard Law School in 1979 to receive a J.D. magna cum laude from Harvard Law School and an M.B.A. from the Harvard Business School, which he pursued at the same time.

From 1980 to 1981, Ogunlesi served as a law clerk to Associate Justice Thurgood Marshall of the United States Supreme Court. Ogunlesi was an attorney in the corporate practice group of the New York City law firm of Cravath, Swaine & Moore, where he had been a summer associate while studying for his M.B.A.

In 1983, Ogunlesi joined the investment bank First Boston as an advisor on a Nigerian gas project. At First Boston, he worked in the Project Finance Group, advising clients on transactions and financings and has worked on transactions in North and South America, the Caribbean, Europe, the Middle East, Africa and Asia. From 1997 to 2002, he was the Head of the Global Energy Group of the then renamed Credit Suisse First Boston (CSFB).

In July 2006, Ogunlesi started the private equity firm, Global Infrastructure Partners (GIP), a joint venture whose initial investors included Credit Suisse and General Electric. He currently serves as Chairman and Managing Partner.

Ogunlesi was appointed to the Board of Directors at Goldman Sachs in 2012 before he was named Lead Director on July 24, 2014.

Ogunlesi served as an adviser, though informally, to Nigerian governments. He was an informal adviser to former President Olusegun Obasanjo on privatization and he still maintains ties with his homeland.

In December 2016, it was announced that Ogunlesi, among other business leaders, would be part of U.S President Donald Trump's Strategic and Policy Forum.

How we can Make Nigeria Work

Earlier, we emphasized a repeating tendency that most of these outstanding Nigerians are based outside Nigeria? This explains the reason why I am so passionate about making Nigeria work. The amount of Nigerians outside the country is less than 1 percent of those in the country, yet we are having such a global impact on the world. What would happen if we fix Nigeria's problems? What will happen if we give similar opportunities to the rest 99 percent of Nigerians living in the country? What kind of result would we then be producing?

What will happen if all the Bayo Ogunlesis in Nigeria are unveiled and empowered within Nigeria? This has been my dream, this is my dream and I am committed to its materialization in my lifetime.

Nigeria indeed can teach the rest of the world!!! Nigeria can be the greatest country on earth.

Personally, I believe that Bayo Ogunlesi is a gold mine for not just Nigeria, but including the rest of Africa.

Ordinarily, one would expect that the Federal Government of Nigeria would have done all within her power to bring a man of such stature back into Nigeria permanently to help turn around the fortunes of the country. Why this is not yet done is a question begging answers.

I want to challenge the government not just to pay lip service to the growth and development of the country. The path for Nigeria to lead the world is clearly defined and is right before us, the government must strive to work with these tested and trusted sons and daughters.

Surely, Bayo Ogunlesi can help administrate within Nigeria another wonder of an airport. He has done it before, why can't he do it again? The government need to see this and work it out.

Again, one pertinent question that is begging for answers is how a Nigerian would run and manage the second largest airport in the world, yet many of our airports across Africa and Nigeria in particular are like Chicken coops and poultry. Why can't we task Bayo Ogunlesi to replicate at least one of such airports in his home country giving him every support needed?

Not only must Bayo Ogunlesi replicate his achievements within Nigeria, he ought to set up a system too that replicates him and develops his kind within our population. Only then would he have built an enduring legacy for himself and the rest of Nigeria.

I strongly believe that our policy makers need to awake for Nigeria to attain to its potential. If a Nigerian can manage the second largest airport in the world, that means Nigeria as a country can own the first, second, third and fourth largest airports in the entire world. It is high time we put a stop to mediocrity. It is high time we stopped eating dung though we are blessed with enormous riches and wealth. It is high time we lived up to our potential and fly.

Nigeria Indeed can Teach the Rest of the World

Bayo Ogunlesi is not alone in this global feat, perhaps we could have deemed his achievements accidental. There other phenomenal Nigerians in same category of outstanding performance. Meet Jude Igwemezie, the Nigerian who constructed a $500 million Iraqi Rail system. Iraq has a solid railway system today, all thanks to the ingenuity of Mr. Jude, a Nigerian.

You are about to read one of the most phenomenal stories of a Nigerian shortly. Like I said, a Nigerian has built Iraq's largest and efficient train system while his own home country does not even have an efficient train system yet.

It is a very sad and disturbing story for Nigeria and Nigerians generally.

Despite the 1.5 billion dollars loan secured from China to construct railway and several billions more for similar projects across the country, our railway system is still till today virtually non existent, due to poor management and mismanagement of funds.

Whereas Kenyas railway system of international standard was built for far less amount.

Nigeria cannot afford to groan in penury if we do not want to kill this country. Right assignments must be given to right men.

When Nigeria has Jude Igwemezie, why not allow the gentleman help reconstruct our rail system?

Nigeria must bring Jude back to help in this task of nation building. Like every similar distinguished Nigerian in diaspora, our greatest ambition right now should be to go back to Nigeria to build a country that our children would be grateful for.

In a later chapter, you will read my personal story and my desire to go back to the land of my birth to contribute to nation building. We all must desire same thing.

So who is this Jude Igwemezie?

Nigerian Constructs $500 Million Iraqi Rail System

Dr. Jude O. Igwemezie, P. Eng., is a registered professional engineer in the province of

Ontario and has been involved with rail related engineering and research since 1981. He obtained his B.Eng. degree in Civil Engineering and M.Eng. and PhD degrees in engineering from McGill University in Montreal, Canada. He is an expert in structural mechanics, stress and failure analyses, design, testing and assessment of railway engineering structures and derailment investigations. Since 1988, his firms have carried out tens of $millions of engineering contracts. He has also authored or co-authored 120 articles, reports and publications on rail track and vehicle systems. Dr. Igwemezie is the Chairman of TransGlobim (Globim) International, and Founder and President of Applied Rail Research technologies (ARRT Inc.), a railway consulting engineering and Research Company and NorFast Inc. that markets premium railway track products developed by ARRT Inc. His clients on the consulting and products sides include all Major Class-1 North American railroads.

Dr. Igwemezie has made significant contributions to the rail industry. He was the first to develop a methodology for setting railhead wear limits. Several North American railroads have successfully implemented his recommendations.

In 1992, he developed and published mathematical relationships between dynamic loads, defect size and rail fracture during cold weather train operations. He has investigated wheel failures in Hi-rail vehicles. He developed the residual stress standards incorporated into the AREMA (American Railway Engineering and Maintenance of Way Association) manual.

Dr. Igwemezie has investigated wheelshelling problems for railroads and suppliers and analyzed wood, concrete and steel tie failures. He has designed derailment containment barriers for residential areas,high relief joint–bar that allow more rail wear for several North American railroads, 124-lb/yd-rail section, new tie plates and clip that fight gauge widening and prevent rail rollover as well as new joint plates that allow positive tie-down of the joint. In 2004, he designed a revolutionary insulated rail joint that has a section modulus that is three times greater than that of current systems and also greater than that of the rail section.

Dr. Igwemezie has been actively involved in the development of track super elevation policies for railroads. Recently, he pioneered development of the software (ASET) for setting track super elevation, locomotive power utilization and fuel optimization in trains. Dr. Igwemezie holds or has pending patents for several innovative railway track components. He has significant experience on the impact of rail grinding and lubrication on: rail life, track forces, rail stresses, tie stresses and track alignment. In 1997, he was invited to address the American Railway Engineering and Maintenance of Way Association (AREMA) on rail management during their annual conference in Chicago. In 2009, he led the team that reorganized the management structure of the Nigerian Railway Corporation. In 1997, the UniP Railroad Steel tie and fastener systems designed by Dr. Igwemezie won the Gold Medal in the Industrial Systems Category of the Canadian Design Engineering Awards. In 2001, Dr. Igwemezie received the "Harry Jerome Award" for Professional Excellence from the Black Business & Professional Association of Canada.

In 2008, he received an Outstanding Business Achievement Award from the Business Development Bank of Canada. In 2009, he received an Award from the Nigerians in Diaspora Organisation (NIDO) Canada for outstanding contributions to the diaspora community and industrialization in Nigeria. In 2009, he also received "Resolution of Appreciation" from the International Heavy Haul Association (IHHA) for his contribution to the latest book on "Best Practices for Heavy Haul Railway Operation". Dr. Igwemezie is also an industry expert on derailments and track component failures including providing expert reports and witness testimony in court litigations.

In 2003, Jude Igwemezie was commissioned by the Iraqi government to design and construct a $500 million Iraqi Rail system.

The contract was to construct what is described as "a viable rail transportation network" for the city of Najaf.

The network connects three Islamic holy and historic mosques in Imam Ali, Kufa and Sahle.

Igwemezie described the rail as the project of its time which he completed in three years, and also built in two phases. "*The first phase, covered the design, construction and operation of the system while the second and final phase will involve the expansion of the system and its extension to the Najaf airport*", he said. Dr Jude is saddled to manage the rail project in Iraq for the next fifty years.

Again, this seem unbelievable considering the fact that Nigeria itself has no functional railway system. This is not only sad but also embarrassing. Experts of nation building have described Nigeria as one nation who is not ready to grow, but can grow and become a world leading power within the shortest time possible whenever she is ready.

This again places emphasis on the need to bring men like Jude into Nigeria for urgent work of rebuilding key sectors.

So as you can see, the tools lie with us. We have the responsibility in our hands. What else are we waiting for?

I came across a brilliant piece beautifully written by a Nigerian on Platform Times, an Online magazine whose name I couldn't readily identify. He described his recent journey to the United States of recent in the article. Permit me to reproduce here a part of what he wrote.

When Nigerians Arise

An event organized by a friend took me to the city of Atlanta a few years ago. The host protocol team had been at the airport 30 minutes before my arrival. I didn't have to wait to be driven to my hotel. Two young people, a man and a woman, were my chaperons. The guy behind the wheel was a 33-year-old medical doctor; so was the 29-year-old young woman who accompanied him. They were both Nigerians.

Venue of the event was packed with about 300 people. Attendees were mostly young Nigerian professionals. A few of them were in the US military running big global operations for the government. Upon their doggedly dependable and broad shoulders, the present and future of a nation were seated. By the time my host got through introducing me to about 20 of the guests who were mainly medical doctors, surgeons, anesthesiologists, researchers, computer scientists, lawyers, and all manner of engineers who were behind the construction of many of the big bridges and roads stretching around America, my heart began to bleed for Nigeria. Some of them were brought into the US by their parents at very tender ages; and others are natural-born US citizens. But all of their hearts yearned for motherland; a place they may never recognize or call home.

This is the story of Nigeria and Nigerians abroad. Young and old doing great exploits in their careers and scattered all over major cities all over the world. Presidents of foreign nations count on them; so do governors of states. Multi-billion dollar corporations desire them; so do small upcoming businesses. These men and women come from all ethnic backgrounds; and their hearts pant for Nigeria; a nation blessed with men and endowed with means.

Recently, a Houston hospital witnessed a handful of Nigerian doctors successfully separating 10-month-old conjoined twins in a 26-hour surgery that is now making waves among American media and the global medical world. The 12-man medical team comprised of Professor. Oluyinka Olutoye, his anesthesiologist wife, Dr. Toyin, and one Dr. Mrs. Oluyemisi Adeyemi-Fowode, a paediatric gynaecology fellow in the hospital. Don't tell me Nigeria doesn't have men.

A Nigerian engineer, Jude Igwemezie (that I just mentioned) who lives in Canada was commissioned by the Iraqi government to design and construct a $500m Iraqi rail system. The project includes the construction of what is described as a viable rail transport network for the city of Najaf. Men who build roads, tunnels and bridges for other nations have been chased away from their homeland by something or someone.

Jelani Aliyu (who has been invited back to Nigeria by the Nigerian government as I earlier wrote) from Sokoto State is the talented mind behind the design of the Chevrolet Volt automobile, one of the most admired American specifications globally.

Aliyu was a senior creative designer with General Motors in Detroit. This Nigerian just made history. I also read about the exploits of one Dr. Osato Osemwengie from Benin, Edo State. Osato specialises in counter-terrorism and counter-insurgence with drones he built for the US Army. His ingenuity makes surveillance and information gathering against terrorists and insurgents easier for the government. Osato lives in the US; and what was a loss to Nigeria became a gain for America.

Amidst all manner of challenges in Nigeria, some Nigerians resident in Nigeria have always towered up in the world. Aliko Dangote, worth $11.7bn, is the richest black man on the face of the earth. The richest black woman on earth is a Nigerian. She is Folorunsho Alakija who is worth almost $2bn. Largest black-owned Communication installation in the world, GLO, is owned by Mike Adenuga, a Nigerian whose net worth is $6.3bn. Nigerians around the world are creators of solutions to world's problems; not designers of problems. There are millions of Nigerians all around the world who have become stand-out achievers and accomplishers of big dreams. Many of them chose to be quiet. We are further convinced that Nigeria is blessed with men.

The country also has the means to kick-start life worth living for all. Nigeria's present GDP is $415bn. "Prophets" in Economics have told us that by 2030, the GDP will jump to around $1tn! This is a sign of means. Between 1999 and 2007, former President Olusegun Obasanjo's administration earned N17tn from crude oil sales within eight years and left behind $45bn external reserves and $3.348bn external debt. Umaru Yar'Adua made N9tn from crude oil sales within the short period he reigned. He grew the reserves to $64bn within just one year. Goodluck Jonathan's administration witnessed an oil boom when Brent crude sold for over $100/barrel, with the regime earning N51tn within a period of five years. The Treasury Single Account policy which was started in February 2015 has reportedly helped save over some N3tn. The Minister of State for Petroleum Resources, Dr Ibe Kachikwu, has also reportedly saved N1.4tn since removing the subsidy on petrol. By year-end 2015, the Customs mopped up almost N1tn from duties and levies. In the month of August this year alone, it generated N95bn. Nigeria is a nation with means.

Many of us are just perturbed that talents, abilities and means that Nigeria and Nigerians exhibit have not translated into good roads, functional hospitals, uninterrupted power supplies, cutting-edge educational system, and plenteous and affordable food supply in our markets. With these blessings, why are we not better than this? In the latest United Nations Human Development Index 2015 Notice, Nigeria ranked 152 out of 188 and adjudged among Low Human Development countries. According to the CBN, between 2014 and 2015, Nigeria spent a total of N1.18tn (about $7.4bn) on the importation of toothpicks, fish, milk, textiles, rice and furniture. Fish imports gulped $1.39bn while milk and rice imports accounted for $1.33bn and $51m respectively. It is obvious that we have the means that are heedlessly frittered away in waste.

Very few Nigerians should go to bed hungry; unfortunately, 120 million people probably will tonight. Chinese teacher and philosopher Confucius once said, *"In a country well-governed, poverty is something to be ashamed of"*. Nelson Mandela, ascending the saddle as head of the South Africa Government, made a vow to his people: *"we pledge ourselves to liberate our people from the bondage of poverty, deprivation, suffering..."*. Poverty is bondage.

What things are inhibiting the growth of Nigeria? Illiteracy, Poor youth empowerment, low human development, corruption, lack of diversification and many more. Again, I have elaborated on each of this in another book titled "WHY COUNTRIES FAIL".

The panacea for all these I have mentioned is responsible citizenship, right policies, involvement of all Nigeriansin nation building, systems overhaul, Propagation of our diversity, education of our citizens etc.

Hope for Nigeria

I am hoping that the coming years in Nigeria will be better and fairer for Nigerians now living under the present harsh economic realities. I hope that all the figures and puzzles strung together by President Buhari and subsequent presidents will eventually translate into sweet dreams for the people now in a nightmare. Although pain and suffering are dominant in the air, I am still hopeful that this administration in the next two and a half years will be able to dig the country out of the hole she has found herself. Nigeria has the requisite men and means to get it done.

Yes, I am hopeful. I am hopeful that Nigeria will rise from the current ashes to her full might and rule the world. I am hopeful that we will become the greatest single entity on earth. I am hopeful that we are the rising sun of the world.

If we will arise to fulfill our innate prophecy, we will maximize the potential of our young people, our intelligent minds, our resourcefulness, then Nigeria will demonstrate to the world a level of prosperity that no other nation in the world at any time has experienced. This is what will happen soon.

Mr. Igwemezie said he was involved in Negotiation with Nigerian officials for more than 18 months to construct several rail lines in the country without success, he disclosed that it took *"only two months to get the Memorandum of Understanding (MoU) executed with Iraqi officials"*. Can you as a Nigerian imagine that?

What took the Iraqi officials just two months to seal with a foreigner, our own government repelled one of their own for more than eighteen months.

Hinting at his frustration to offer his services to Nigeria, Mr. Igwemezie said, *"as a Diaspora person, I kept coming back, knocking, to help Nigeria. On the other hand I can't knock forever"*.

Mr. Igwemezie, who wants to build a standard gauge railway system from Lagos to Calabar, believes that Nigeria is a place where railway service is going to be *"profitable and successful because of its size and population and because we have a demography similar to that in Europe"*. However, he said, the bane of railway in Nigeria is that *"we have brought the wrong people to help us"*.

Do you now see the reason why the experts described Nigeria as not being ready to grow? When we are ready, the world will witness the most rapid growth of a Nation it had ever seen.

I challenge our government to wake up. I challenge every one of us to wake up. We cannot continue to dance the dance of shame forever. We must stand up now and build. Why will the other countries of the world continue to benefit from the magnanimity and ingenuity of the Ogunlesis and the Igwemezies of Nigeria.

It will cost the Nigerian government little to nothing to bring back Jude Igwemezie into the country and saddle him with the responsibility of transforming the rail system in Nigeria. Jude Igwemezie can be given the opportunities to build his company within Nigeria. Jude Igwemezie can be supported and given targets or projects to accomplish within a stipulated time. Jude Igwemezie can develop many of the Nigerian projects same way he is doing that for many countries of the world. Nigeria must now arise and become the greatest nation on earth.

More than Bayo Ogunlesi and building large airports, more than Jude Igwemezie building exceptional rail lines, how about a Nigerian building an exceptional opposition party in a foreign country. Yes, have you heard of that? Her name is Helen Mukoro.

Helen Mukoro: Forcing a Nation to Grow

There is a Nigerian lady whose name is making the rounds in Spain, it is no one other than Nigerian born Spanish lawyer, Helen Mukoro, who has emerged the presidential candidate of an opposition party for the 2015 presidential election in Spain.

Helen is said to have set a new record as the first woman and an immigrant to emerge presidential flag bearer of a political party in Spain. She will be running on the platform of Union De Todos, a party she founded earlier this year. The forensic expert and author of many books, was born in Delta state and worked briefly in the governor's office before she travelled to Spain in 1992, where She gained prominence in Spanish politics. She came into full glare, when she instituted a political party and later became the first Nigerian-Spanish to contest for the Mayor of Denia in May this year, an election which she lost. However, her popularity soared higher after her loss, as many people endorsed her for the highest office in the land.

Aside graduating in Law at the Spanish National University Alicante, Helen holds several academic qualifications. She holds a masters degree in criminology, masters degree in social education, a post graduate certificate in tax and labor management, a post graduate certificate in forensic psychology, and a post graduate certificate in Immigration and Domestic Violence. A very experienced personnel, Helen worked as a legal consultant (immigration department) at the Red Cross Society, Spain and presently owns a legal firm. She served as the CEO and President at the African Europe Chamber of Commerce. CEO/President at National Agency of Forensic Experts, Mediators and Technical Professionals of Spain and Europe. This dynamic Nigerian dame has been fingered as one following the footsteps of the United States President, Barack Obama, who was the first African-American to win the presidency.

Helen has taught Nigeria on so many grounds on how to become the greatest nation in the world. Firstly, women must not be sidelined in any society. The progress of many nations rests firmly on the lean but firm shoulders of women who have proven consistently that they are co-partners in the journey to progress. As a matter of fact, the development of Europe as a continent can be traced to the impact of many strong women holding the frontiers of their nations, from Margaret Thatcher of decades ago in Great Britain to current day Angela Merkel of Germany.

If Nigeria must become the greatest country in the world as she is bound to be, then women at all levels must be deployed for national development. No woman must be looked down upon. If Helen Mukoro in faraway Spain can launch and effectively run a popular opposition party, then it is a clarion call for the women of Nigeria.

Additionally, Helen Mukoro has demonstrated yet again the power in Nigerians and the role the opposition party must play in the development of a nation. We all do not need to agree and be clustered together in same views, but we can harness our different views through constructive criticisms to grow a nation. I can only hope that this message comes across well.

Helen Mukoro, is leading a political revolution in a foreign land, but she is not the only one doing this. Have you heard the incredible story of Taofick, leading a global Barbie-revolution? Yes, a very unusual form of revolution.

When a Nigerian made Doll Outsells Barbie, now that is a Revolution!

As Barbie sales continue to plummet all over the world, another doll is aiming to slide in and take her place. The Queens of Africa and Naija Princess dolls are outselling the world's original. The dolls' mastermind, 43-year-old Taofick Okoya, told Reuters that he sells between 6,000 and 9,000 dolls per month, claiming 10 to 15 percent of the small, but growing toy market in Nigeria.

According to Forbes, Taofick said 'I got into the doll business by chance. At that time my daughter was young, and I realized she was going through an identity crisis, she wished she was white, and I was trying to figure out where that came from. I used to always buy her white dolls, and it never got to me that is was relevant which color her dolls were. On top of that, we have DSTV in

Nigeria where children watch the Disney programs, and all her favorite characters were white. I started to understand why she'd feel the way she did, cause it was all that she'd been exposed to,' the 'Queens of Africa' dolls creator explains.

Upon realizing the non-existence of black dolls within the Nigerian market, he decided to create a brand of his own. The dolls' body parts are manufactured in China, and are subsequently assembled in Nigeria. In the midst of it all, Taofick also empowers local communities of stay-at-home mothers, who make money off of braiding the dolls' hair and creating outfits. 'It takes about three hours braiding the hair. One of these women has made 60,000 Naira (roughly $300) doing this.'

The physical features of his dolls are a constant work in progress, and Okoya aims at bringing changes to the dolls' looks every two years.

The World's Sunset and Sunrise

That story of Taofick reminds me of the analogy we gave in a previous chapter about the SUN SET and the SUN RISE of the world. America is the world's sun set, Nigeria is the world's sun rise. For anybody that cares to listen, Nigeria is going to be known as the rising star of the future world!

This I am absolutely convinced about. Nigerians are not people of a small stature by any dimension. Nigerians are filled with so much strength, grace and power. Nigerians are achievers, Nigerians are some of the greatest people you will find on the surface of the earth.

We must bring all of these opportunities together to build for ourselves the greatest country in the world.

It is interesting to see how building a nation can become incredibly easy when the emphasis is on mind development, education and human capacity training.

For this to become a reality however, that emphasis must not just be the responsibility of the government, it must be the emphasis of all stakeholders within a nation. For example, religious houses, families and the general society must all sing same song. We all must emphasize the need to grow our minds as a matter of urgency.

You will remember that while we looked at the Jewish stories briefly in an earlier chapter, we saw how the Jews changed their emphasis and goal to tailor into what they want to experience and see as a nation. It therefore is no surprise at all that the Jews are one of the strongest nations in the world today. Their Human Development Index is quite high.

Building Nigeria is not rocket science. Building a nation is not as difficult as it seems. If we have one Nigerian who has been able to do it, we need to invest in him. We need him to replicate himself at least in a thousand other children. We need to celebrate him. He must become the icon that everyone sees on the Television and he must be the one being listened to on radio stations. He must become very popular in our schools and colleges. He must become the role model for our children. It is very shameful that millions of Nigerian children do not know the names I have cited so far in this book. It is shameful and disgraceful. We need to invest in these young people rightly and appropriately if we must become the greatest nation in the world.

Taofick has done it and we have seen his story. Taofick's idea is unique in the sense that children will always be born hence he will always have a large potential market for his products.

Taking Taofick's case as an example, what exactly do young people mean when they say there are no jobs, or that Nigeria is barren? What exactly do they need when they are trying to smuggle their way out of Nigeria. Many of our graduates are not aware that the best place for them to prosper is within Nigeria. Where there are lot of problems, there are lots of opportunities. We must begin to change the way we think and our perspectives. Nigeria indeed, can become the greatest country in the world.

Nothing is going to stop us now. This is our destiny and we must fulfill it.

NUGGETS

- I challenge our government to wake up.
- If Nigeria must become the greatest country in the world as she is bound to be, then women at all levels must be deployed for national development.
- America is the world's sun set, Nigeria is the world's sun rise.
- We must bring all of the opportunities in Nigeria together to build for ourselves the greatest country in the world.
- Building Nigeria is not rocket science. Building a nation is not as difficult as it seems.
- If we have one Nigerian who has been able to do something incredible, we need to invest in him.
- Where there are lot of problems, there are lots of opportunities. We must begin to change the way we think and our perspectives.

CHAPTER SIX

UNUSUAL NIGERIAN FAMILIES

In the last chapter, we saw how Nigerians are raining major exploits on certain communities and nations of the world. We also observed that making Nigeria the greatest country in the world is easier than many of us think. So far in this book, I have given examples of certain exploits that certain Nigerians are doing that no other person has been able to replicate in the world.

Just because I am committed to giving you many more outstanding proofs, in this chapter we are going to look some of the greatest stories you will ever come across in the world. In fact, do you know that some of the most outstanding families in the world are Nigerians? One of such phenomenal families is the Imafidon family.

The Smartest Family in the World is Nigerian

The Imafidons, a Nigerian family based in UK have popularly been dubbed "Britain's Smartest Family" and the "World's smartest family" as the family is made up of geniuses and prodigies. They have also been said to have broken lots of world records.

Dr. Chris Imafidon who is the patriarch of the Imafidon family and Ann Imafidon are blessed with five gifted children whose names are Anne-Marie Imafidon 27, Christina Imafidon 23, Samantha 19 and the 16-year-old twins Peter and Paula Imafidon.

He is currently working as a renowned scholar and international education consultant to several governments. He also serves as a mentor and coach to American students at various academic levels using Skype and web technology.

Here are his children and their exploits:

1. **Anne-Marie Imafidon:** In 2003, Anne-Marie Imafidon became the youngest person to pass the UK A-level computing exam when she was only 13. She went on to attend John Hopkins University in Baltimore and received her master's degree from Oxford University, all before she turned 20 thereby making her the youngest graduate ever to attain a master's degree from Oxford University at age 19. She specialized in Mathematics and Computer Science.

Now 27, Anne-Marie speaks six languages and currently works as an enterprise collaboration strategist at Deutsche Bank in the UK. She is also the founder of Stemettes, to inspire the next generation of women into science, technology, engineering and mathematics (S.T.E.M) program.

In 2017, Queen Elizabeth II, awarded Nigeria's Anne-Marie Imafidon an MBE, Member of the Order of the British Empire, for her work inspiring the next generation of women in Science, Technology, Engineering and Mathematics (STEM). According to reports, at 27, Imafidon is the youngest scientist to get a royal recognition since 1890.

More than anything, Imafidon serves as a role model to young girls who would otherwise have been unable to see a female figure excelling in the industry. Her organisation has tutored and mentored about 15,000 girls across the UK, Ireland and Europe; proof that she is deserving of the honour of an MBE.

2. **Christiana Imafidon:**

At 11 years old, Christina Imafidon (now 23) was the youngest student in history to ever get accepted and study at an undergraduate institution at any British university at the tender age of 11. Christina is now working as an intern with the Citigroup Corporation as well as conducting research on mathematics with Oxford University.

3. **Samantha Imafidon:**

19-year-old Samantha Imafidon had passed two high school-level mathematics and statistics exams at age 6. She became the youngest girl in the UK to attend secondary school at the age of 9.

Samantha was the sibling who mentored the twins to pass their own math secondary school test when they were also 6 years old. She is a gold level champion in the 100m and 200m relays.

4. **Peter and Paula Imafidon:**

The twins Peter and Paula Imafidon are nicknamed “The Wonder Twins”, Peter and Paula are Great Britain's current highest achievers. At 9-years-old they made history as the youngest children in British history to attend high school.

They astounded veteran experts of academia when they became the youngest to ever pass the University of Cambridge's advanced mathematics exam.

They set world records when they passed the A/AS-level math papers. Peter Imafidon, who is also a 100m and 400m relay champ in London, has said that he would like to serve as Prime Minister one day and his sister Paula, a country champion in rugby, would like to teach math to students.

Dr Imafidon strongly believes that anyone can achieve what he has achieved with his family through a specific model for education.

In his own family, if one child had a reading assignment, there was a communal effort. *"If you really want a child to learn anything, find out the best way that child learns,"* says Imafidon. *"Every human being has a unique way of learning."*

Do you agree any less that Nigeria is the greatest country in the world? The Imafidons exemplify the thousands of home we have in Nigeria at the moment. The only difference is that the Imafidons have been able to harness that potential using the information and environment at their disposal.

If we will act rightly, that time is soon upon us that every Nigerian home will be like that of the Imafidons.

So what do we need to do to actualize this? The Imafidons believe that it is not too hard to replicate themselves and their kind of global achievements. As a personal friend and someone I have worked with closely for years, I have seen Prof Chris Imafidon replicate what he has done with his own kids with several other children and young adults too.

So again what do we need to do in order to raise thousands of Imafidons in Nigeria?

Task for the Government of Nigeria

The Nigerian government must endeavor to bring the Imafidon family into Nigeria and let them set up in Nigeria to bring out and develop stars. Ann-Marie, the first child of the Imafidons in her own right has raised more than 15,000 girls for science and technology already. I believe that given the structure and support she needs, Ann-Marie can raise several thousands of girls who will be problem solvers of our society in Nigeria. While she has been awarded an MBE by the queen of England, she is yet to be recognized by the government of her own country.

Prof. Chris Imafidon is already a consultant to governments of many countries especially in Europe and America. One would expect that it is around such men our educational apparatus as a country would be built on. There is no gainsaying the fact that this man has what it takes to turn the educational fortunes of Nigeria around forever. The question begging answers right now is why we are not maximizing his abilities yet.

The diaspora is a ready tool to develop Nigeria. Using the diaspora to develop Nigeria is a fast track to becoming the greatest country in the world. We need to set up structures that maximize the best brains especially those children that are the best in world Universities. They need contracts that will help them develop their ideas and projects and become the best. Same goes for all the talents including the football stars, athletes, tennis stars etc.

Dear readers, now I hope you are beginning to agree with me that Nigeria is on its way to teach the rest of the world and become the greatest nation on earth?

You cannot read the incredible story of the Imafidons and not be excited about the potential that Nigeria has. Do we have more like them? Well, do you know the family with the most Chartered accountants in the world is also Nigerian?

Most Chartered Accountants in one Family

According to the Guinness book of World records, the Nigerian family of David Omueya Dafinone have broken the record of having the highest number of chartered accountants in one family in the world.

Three sons and two daughters of Senator David Omueya and Cynthia Esella Dafinone of Lagos, Nigeria, all qualified as members of the Institute of Chartered Accountants in England and Wales between 1986 and 1999. Their father had also become a member of the same institution in 1963. Igho Omueya Dafinone, Ede Omueya Dafinone and Duvie Omueya Dafinone are currently working within the firm of D O Dafinone Co. Chartered Accontants in Lagos. Daphne Omueya Dafinone and Joy Ufuoma Dafinone live in London.

Senator David Omueya Dafinone, 88, is an accomplished accountant, administrator and erudite politician. The patriarch of the Dafinone family, an accounting family listed in the Guinness book of records as having the largest number of accountants in one family, is the proprietor of D.O Dafinone & Company, which he founded in 1966 and later merged to become Horwath Dafinone and Company.

Born on March 12, 1927 in Sapele, Delta State, Dafinone announced his arrival on Nigeria's political landscape with his landslide victory in Bendel South Senatorial election in 1979 when he was 52 years old. Then Delta was under defunct Bendel State, which has now been broken into two - Edo and Delta. Running on the platform of the National Party of Nigeria, NPN, he polled 59,632 votes to beat Thompson Salubi of the Unity Party of Nigeria, UPN (24,874 votes) and E.E.E Idigbo of the Great Nigeria Peoples Party, GNPP (20,760 votes). Elder statesman As a senator, Dafinone, who owns the Ceddi Plaza, Abuja, was one of the leaders of the movement for the creation of Delta State in the 1980s and the efforts yielded dividends in 1991. The nationalist, who is a member of The Patriots, a group of eminent elder statesmen, of late, has been leading the Union of Niger Delta, a non governmental environmental and social justice pressure group.

His humanitarian service manifest in various forms, particularly his pivotal role in the construction of the Orodje of Okpe's palace, a project that was completed in 1997. He has also been functioning as Chairman and Patron of sundry bodies in Okpe Kingdom. In recognition of his immense and selfless contributions to the socio-economic and political development of Okpe Kingdom, he was honoured in 1997 with the traditional title of Owhere 1 of Okpe Kingdom by the Orodje of Okpe.

An award of Certificate of Excellence for professional practice by the Delta State Government was also given to Senator Dafinone in September 1997. In 2001, he was awarded the ICAN Certificate of Merit for Outstanding contributions to the Accounting profession by the institute of Chartered Accountant of Nigeria. And in 2003, the Federal Government conferred on him the National Honour of the Officer of the Federal Republic, OFR. On August 1, 2000, Guinness World Records recognized Senator Dafinone as the patriarch of the Family with the highest number of Chartered Accountants (who are members of the Institute of Chartered Accountants in England Wales) in one nuclear family - a recognition that has received resounding ovations from far and wide. In 2006, he received a 'definite entry' in the Cambridge Blue Book for an outstanding contribution in the field of Accountancy. Married to Chief Cynthia Watson Dafinone, like earlier noted, the elder statesman, is blessed with three sons and two daughters. Interestingly, all of them are qualified and chartered accountants, a world record. They all had degrees in Economics. They are all, today working for the same firm, Horwath Dafinone.

Without a shadow of doubt, Nigerians do not make small attempts. Nigerians only attempt big things that places them on the global stage.

I have made much attempts to highlight these incredible men and women so that young people without an idea of the spirit of Nigeria can read and learn. It seems to me that this Nigerian spirit is fast eroding. Nigerians are fast forgetting who we are. We must be careful and not lose touch with our personality.

Nigeria is only Going Through a Challenging Phase

The challenges of today is just a phase in our national life. Like the wind, it will soon pass away when we make attempts at doing the right things. Surely, more Nigerian families can break global records like the Imafidons and the Dafinones. If we have some who have done it, we can have more who can do it. We all can take a cue and learn. We are Nigerians, the nation that is the rising sun of the future.

Moreover, if we have a Nigerian family that is the smartest family in the world, and another Nigerian family that has the most number of Chartered accountants in the world, why then do we have almost a paradox that almost 65 million people are illiterates. According to UNESCO, 65 million Nigerians cannot read and write. Nigeria has a population of about 180 million people. Now, that is so sad because that means currently, more than one-third of Nigerians cannot even be accessed for their potential and capabilities. More than one-third of Nigerians are incapacitated by lack to good education. Can you imagine a nation whose one-third of citizens are largely dependent and cannot optimize their human capacity? I think this is not just a tragedy, it is an emergency.

This is why I am raising a cry through this book to maximize the opportunity that presents itself through the Imafidons and the Dafinones of Nigeria. There is no tenable excuse why Nigeria should have the smartest families in the world and a very high rate of illiterate families in the world at same time.

We must give people with proven results the task of revamping and personalizing our educational system. Education can be made personal for everyone from our small children who we owe the absolute responsibility of access to the best education for the sake of their future to our aged ones who might still be interested in training their minds. Nigeria needs to declare a state of emergency in our educational sector and bring about urgent reforms.

Reinvestment in our human capital must become our priority, Nigeria is wealthy not because of her oil reserves but because of her people. Hence, it is a horrible situation that less than 50% of our people are educated adequately to even help themselves, whereas perhaps much less can read and write. Even the 50% of people who can read and write are not all educated in matters of nation building and need to be reoriented. Many of our so called educated people are still very tribalistic and sorely parochial.

The economy of Nigeria so far is built on less than 20% truly literate people. Why don't we raise the bar to 80%. We must maximize our people especially the young Nigerians. This will make Nigeria become the greatest country in the world in no time

The best bet that Nigeria has to lead the world however, is her young people, which she has in abundance. The trend seems to be whenever Nigerians are given the right environment to function, they tend to exceed their contemporaries and colleagues. I would like to mention a few stories of outstanding young individuals who left the shores of Nigeria to become the best in the various nations they found themselves in.

Exceptional Nigerian Students in World Universities

Emmanuel Ohuabunwa

A 22-year-old Nigerian, Emmanuel Ohuabunwa, made history at John Hopkins University, United States of America. Ohuabunwa from Arochukwu, Abia State, did the nation proud by becoming the first black man to make a Grade Point Average of 3.98 out of 4.0 to bag a degree in Neurosciences in the university. He was also adjudged as having the highest honors during the graduation that was held on May 24 that year.

Tunji Olu-Taiwo

A genius could be referred to as an exceptional child who is academically sound. But, how would you describe an individual who never misses a point in his examinations from first year in the university to the final year? If there is any adjective to qualify such a person, that word could best describe Tunji Olu-Taiwo, an Engineering student of Eastern Mediterranean University in the Turkish Republic of North Cyprus who obtained 4.0 CGPA out of 4.0 CGPA, the first ever in the department.

Ganiyu Sanusi

Over the past five years, Nigerian students at the Russian National Research Medical University have consistently topped the graduation chat, bagging honors and contributing their wealth of knowledge to the University's academic status.

In a Russian University in the year 2012, a Nigerian student, Ganiyu Sanusi bagged the "Best Student of the year" award at the University's quiz competition. He graduated as the best student in the faculty with first-class honors and a CGPA of 5.0.

Another Nigeria-born Alonge Olanike Omotola, who in 2010 represented the country on the Russian national research university hall of fame, bagged first-class honors degree in Medicine and Surgery. She was the best Graduating student and valedictorian for that year.

Uwa Osamede Imafidon

A 24-year-old Nigerian, Uwa Osamede Imafidon, graduated from theUniversity of Texas at Arlington (UTA) in the US with Masters in Microbiology and made a 4.0 CGPA out of the maximum 4.0 CGPA

This is just a small list of incredibly talented young Nigerians that are scattered all over the world pursuing their dreams and proving to be best in their fields. In the next 20 years, these people will be leading the world for sure. Friends, I don't have any doubt in my mind about the place and future of Nigeria among the comity of nations.

Other such young brilliant Nigerians in world universities creating global records include:

Ufot Ekong

In his first semester at Tokai University, Japan, Akwa Ibom native, Ufot Ekong, solved a mathematical puzzle that students have been unable to solve for three decades. The 24year old didn't stop at that, he went on to break a 50 year old academic record by graduating the 'Best

All Rounder' with a first-class degree in electrical engineering, and getting the highest grades the university had witnessed in 50 years.

The remarkable young man didn't achieve these feats on a gold platter, Ekong worked two jobs to pay his tuition through school, and runs a retail wears and accessories shop in Japan called Strictly African Japan.

Osarieme Omonuwa

At 22, Osarieme Anita Omonuwa bagged a first class honour at the University of Reading, United Kingdom, making her the first black woman to win the Reading University Chancellor's Award in the history of the 121-year-old institution.

Just like Ufot Ekong, Omonuwa was awarded a total of six prizes - Student of the year, Best female graduating student, Council of Legal Education Star Prize, amongst others.

Omonuwa has always been a star child, always topping her class, right from her kindergarten days. In the 2008/2009 academic session at the Igbinedion education Centre, Benin City, she took home several prizes, including that of the best graduating student.

On her arrival in the United Kingdom, Omonuwa received the University of Reading scholarship award in 2010, and was also recognized as the best student in the international foundation program.

The 22 year old was once described by her university chancellor, Sir John Madejski, as "a representative of our brightest and best students." And to celebrate Nigeria's centenary in 2014, Osarieme Omonuwa's photographs donned the walls of her institution as a symbol of excellence.

Dr Victor Olalusi

Few years ago, Dr Victor Olalusi was honored by the Federal Ministry of Education Nigeria for being an ambassador of excellence. As a medical student, Olalusi scored a 5.0 Cumulative Grade Point Average (GPA) for seven consecutive years at the Russian National Research Medical University (RNRMU), Moscow. This made him the best graduating student in the whole Russian Federation in 2013.

Olalusi never fell below 5.0 in all the courses he took throughout his course of study, not even in the Russian language class. Prior to achieving this feat, this phenomenal young man had a string of notable achievements - Best WAEC result Nigeria, 2004, Cowbell Award in 2006, Highest Post UME score at the Obafemi Awolowo University (OAU) in 2006, OAU Medicine First Merit list in 2006.

For his astounding academic performance, the RNRMU placed Olalusi in the institution's hall of fame for academic excellence. At the event organized to honour Olalusi, Artem Romanov, a representative of the Russian Embassy, said that Nigerians are blessed with abundant human potential, *"It has been acknowledged in the Russian Ministry of Education that Nigerians have a lot of exceptional talents."*

Oluwatobi Olasunkanmi

24 year old son of former Minister of Youth Development in Nigeria, Oluwatobi Olasunkanmi, was awarded

the William Charnley Prize for excelling at the University of Cambridge, United Kingdom.

Olasunkanmi graduated with the best First Class in Law at the renowned university, and was also the only black student in the graduating set.

Dr Philip Johnson, a senior tutor at the university, congratulated Olasunkanmi. He said *"Many congratulations on obtaining the best Hughes Hall First Class in your BA in Law. In recognition, the College has awarded you with the William Charnley Prize."*

While we are still on this discussion about the factor of the Nigerian spirit, especially as it causes our young people to excel in academics globally, there is a young man you need to know about. Please meet, 22 year old Emmanuel Ohuabunwa.

Emmanuel Ohuabunwa

Not only did he graduate top of his class at Johns Hopkins University, he made history by becoming the first black man to do so in the university's history!

Johns Hopkins University is acclaimed worldwide as a leading university in the field of medicine. It pioneered the concept of modern research in the United States and has ranked among the world's top such universities throughout its history. The National Science Foundation has ranked the university #1 among U.S. academic institutions in total science, medical and engineering research and development and as at 2011, about 37 Nobel Prize winners have been affiliated with the University.

Oyeleye Lateefah

Oyeleye Lateefah Abiola, a native of Ibadan, Oyo state, Nigeria and a scholarship student has emerged as the best graduating medical student overall in her class of 2017 topping her 564 peers with a percentage score of 95.6% in Ukraine. She is one of the 87 students sponsored by the Osun state government to study Medicine at the National University of Kharkiv, Ukraine.

The brilliant 25 year old doctor says "*When I found out I had the best result in the Krok 2 medical exam, it felt unreal at first, then I felt really happy and proud of my achievement, then the pressure came, knowing the amount of work I still have ahead of me. But generally I'm happy that I finally proved to myself that hard work pays.*"

Ado Abdulkadir

A Nigerian undergraduate student, Ado Abdulkadir, won an Indian music reality show competition, after defeating over 8,000 native Indians to their own music and dance. Can you believe that?

The Kano-born youth, whose spectacular outings surprised spectators and the judges, joined more than 8,000 Indians in the Sa Re Ga Ma Pa song and dance competition which he went on to win.

The video clip of Abdulkadir, dancing and singing Indian music kitted in Indian attire, went viral on social media with several thousands of views.

But in an interview with BBC, Abdulkadir, said his performances in the competition, as the first African to reach the last 17 stage, is beginning to positively affect the perception of Nigerians amongst Indians.

"More than 8,700 people entered the competition, but presently I am one of the last 17 people that have remained in the competition.

I am the first African to be in this competition. After every week, two people are being dropped. That is how we now become 17, out of thousands that started.

The final, where the winner will emerge, is when people remain only five in the competition," he said.

Abdulkadir went to India, under the Indian Council for Cultural Relations (ICCR) to study Computer Application, few years ago.

"It all started with my interest in Indians, because I nurtured the passion to learn the language ever since I was 14.

And as the passion continued, I then met one, Mr Zubairu in Abuja, where I was based, who translates Hindi language to English. That has helped me tremendously to where I am today. He was the one who helped me, indeed. I learnt a number of Hindi words from him," he said.

Ado later went on to win the competition.

The height of accomplishments of these young Nigerians in the world is a strong proof that indeed Nigeria is the rising sun of the future.

50 Nigerian Students In Malaysia

With the graduation of 253 Nigerians from various academic disciplines at the 2015 convocation ceremony of the Linton University College Malaysia, 50 made first class honours.

Altogether 50 Nigerian graduates distinguished themselves with first class honours degrees, among whom were 13 PTDF scholars who earned first class degrees in Software Engineering, Mechanical Engineering, Electrical and Electronic Engineering, Business Management and Civil Engineering.

The Acting High Commissioner of Nigeria to Malaysia, Mrs. Janet Odeka, said in a statement, that the unprecedented achievement of the Nigerian scholars in the university in Malaysia had contributed in creating a positive image for Nigerians living in the country.

Mrs Odeka said, *"I am really excited and grateful because this is the first time we are having such number of graduates who produced good results such as first class and second class upper. We have had students from Nigeria who were involved in criminal activities and other immoral acts, but for the first time we are celebrating something we should be proud of as Nigerians and I wish to appeal to Nigerians here that they should emulate what these graduands have done to attract a good name for Nigeria."*

While all of these Nigerians are brilliantly excelling in many universities in the world, not many people also know that Nigeria has the fourth largest number of medical doctors in the world with the number ever increasing according to the world Facts book. What this means is that Nigeria will continually have a pool of professionals she can use to advance herself. Not only is there an increasing number of doctors in the country, other professionals such as engineers, teachers, nurses, accountants, lawyers etc.

To conclude this chapter and to highlight the brilliant mind of Nigerians once more, you must meet the Nigerian doctor who is the first black chairperson of the

United states cardiovascular board, reputed to be the biggest cardiovascular board in the world.

Nigerian Doctor who is the First Black Person to Chair us Cardiovascular Disease Board

The man who is responsible for certifying all deserving cardiologists in the United States is a Nigerian.

For the first time, since its inception, 81 years ago, the American Board of Internal Medicine (ABIM) has appointed a black person as head of its cardiovascular disease board. And not only is he black, he is also a Nigerian doctor. Dr Olakunle Akinboboye as chair of the board will now be in charge of certifying cardiologists in the United States. The board which has 12 members across the United States will be headed by Dr Akinboboye, who will also have to carry out periodic knowledge assessments of all practicing cardiologists in the US.

Akinboboye received his medical degree from the College of Medicine at the University of Ibadan, Nigeria and later finished his internal medicine residency and part of his cardiology fellowship at the Nassau County Medical Center, State University of Stony Brook. He has master's degrees in public health from Columbia University and business administration from Columbia Business School. He completed his fellowship in cardiology with two years of dedicated training in nuclear cardiology and advanced echocardiography, when he moved to Columbia University.

Certified in cardiovascular disease, hypertension and sleep medicine, this won't be his first board appointment. Akinboboye serves as chair of the clinical trials committee of the organisation and also on the international board of governors of the American college of cardiology as the liaison for Africa.

He is an associate professor of clinical medicine at the Weill Medical College of Cornell University in New York, the medical director of Queens Heart Institute/ Laurelton Heart specialist in Rosedale, Queens, New York and a past-president of the National Association of Black Cardiologists' (ABC).

He won an award for "exemplary professional services and outstanding contributions to cardiovascular medicine" while serving as president of the Ibadan College of Medicine alumni association, North America, between 2004-2005.

Dr Akinboboye is a glory to Nigeria. This unusual doctor has proven yet again what the future of Nigeria looks like, a future where Nigeria leads and heads in all things.

Again, I desire that the government of Nigeria will work together with this unusual doctor to revive especially our failing health services in Nigeria notably the field of cardiology. When this is done, our politicians will no longer need to travel around the world for simple ailments.

When Nigerian Teenage Girls Solve Global Problem

A team of four Nigerian girls has created a generator that produces six hours of electricity using only a single liter of urine as fuel.

According to a report by Forbes, Four teenage girls figured out a way to use a liter of urine as fuel to get six hours of electricity from their generator. Fourteen-year-olds Duro-Aina Adebola, Akindele Abiola, and Faleke Oluwatoyin, and 15-year-old Bello Eniola displayed their invention at Maker Faire Africa in Lagos, Nigeria, an annual event meant to showcase ingenuity.

Here's how the urine-powered generator works:

- Urine is put into an electrolytic cell, which separates out the hydrogen.
- The hydrogen goes into a water filter for purification, and then into a gas cylinder, which looks similar to the kind used for outdoor barbecue grills.
- The gas cylinder pushes the filtered hydrogen into another cylinder that contains liquid borax, in order to remove moisture from the gas. Borax is a natural mineral, commonly used in laundry detergent.
- The hydrogen is pushed into a power generator in the final step of the process.

A big drawback is that hydrogen poses an explosion risk. But the girls used one-way valves throughout the device as a safety measure.

The idea of using urine as fuel is not new. The girls have come up with a practical way to put the idea into action, though. Their method for using urine to power a generator is one the average household can appreciate.

Power generators are used far more often in Africa. Power outages happen multiple times a day in Lagos, so all those who can afford a backup generator have one.

Still, technology needs to evolve further before such a system is feasible, at least as far as applications like powering generators go.

Gerardine Botte, a professor of chemical and biomolecular engineering at Ohio University, is among those working on practical ways to make urine into a more useful hydrogen source, essentially by turning power into a byproduct of wastewater treatment. She says it takes more energy to extract hydrogen from urine than you end up getting in return as electricity. The energy equation gets even more skewed by the inefficiency of the generator used in the girls' project.

"At first glance, they're not having a net gain in energy," Botte says. *"But I think it's important to say that these little girls, trying to do something like this, deserve a lot of credit."*

By and large, we have explored extensively the mind and educational potential of Nigeria in this chapter. We have seen that when it comes to intelligence rating, Nigeria is not just going to be the intelligence capital of the world, it is already the intelligence capital of the world. This we have seen through the numerous examples that I have given already.

We need to arise and maximize the educational industry to build for ourselves the greatest country in the world. I see in the distant future, when men and women from all the six continents of the world will strive to get an admission into our schools and colleges in Nigeria. That time is near, and that time is now.

NUGGETS

- We must give people with proven results the task of revamping and personalizing our educational system.
- We must maximize our people especially the young Nigerians.
- The best bet that Nigeria has to lead the world is her young people
- The height of accomplishments of young Nigerians around the world is a strong proof that indeed Nigeria is the rising sun of the future.
- Nigeria has the fourth largest number of medical doctors in the world with the number ever increasing according to the world Facts book.
- Nigeria is not just going to be the intelligence capital of the world, it is already the intelligence capital of the world.
- We need to arise and maximize the educational industry to build for ourselves the greatest country in the world.

CHAPTER SEVEN

HOW TO MAKE NIGERIA STRONGER USING THE ELITES

In the final chapters of this book, I want to show you the enormous wealth that we have as Nigerians to build our nation economically.

You remember vividly that in the last chapter, we had serious discussions on the quality of minds Nigerians possess and how to build the greatest nation on earth using our human capital. Right now, I want to show you ready tools with which we can drastically turn around the fortunes of our dear country.

A ready tool that Nigeria can tap into in the development of her Human capital is the enormous wealth of her wealthiest citizens. Like we already saw earlier in this book, certain Nigerians have excelled tremendously outside the shores of Nigeria due to the environment that favors their growth and productivity. Now, certain Nigerians have also excelled within the country. In fact, as at the time of writing this book, the richest black man and the richest black woman on earth are Nigerians. What a feat for a country that some ignorant people have termed poor.

If Nigeria is really poor, the richest black man and the richest black woman on earth wouldn't be found within her borders. Therefore, what that means is that if Nigeria has the richest black man and the richest black woman in the world, this country definitely has to be among the richest in the world and the best place to be.

How then has Nigeria been able to produce the richest black man and woman in the world, closely followed by some of the richest men and women in Africa and the world? A close look into their stories might help solve some of the riddles.

Aliko Dangote: the Richest Black Man in the World

Aliko Dangote GCON (born 10 April 1957) is a billionaire, who owns the Dangote Group, which has interests in commodities. The company operates in Nigeria and other African countries, including Benin, Ethiopia, Senegal, Cameroon, Ghana, South Africa, Togo, Tanzania, and Zambia. As of February 2017, he had an estimated net worth of US$12.5 billion.

Dangote is ranked by Forbes magazine as the 67th richest person in the world and the richest man in Africa; he peaked on the list as the 23rd richest person in the world in 2014. He surpassed Saudi-Ethiopian billionaire Mohammed Hussein Al Amoudi in 2013 by over $2.6 billion to become the world's richest black man.

Dangote hails from a very prominent business family that has lived in Nigeria for many years. He is the great grandson of Alhaji Alhassan Dantata, the richest

African at the time of his death in 1955. Dangote said, *"I can remember when I was in primary school, I would go and buy cartons of sweets [sugar boxes] and I would start selling them just to make money. I was so interested in business, even at that time."*

The Dangote Group was established as a small trading firm in 1977, the same year Dangote relocated to Lagos to expand the company. Today, it is a multi-trillion naira conglomerate with many of its operations in Benin, Ghana, Nigeria, and Togo. Dangote has expanded to cover food processing, cement manufacturing, and freight. The Dangote Group also dominates the sugar market in Nigeria and is a major supplier to the country's soft drink companies, breweries, and confectioners. The Dangote Group has moved from being a trading company to being the largest industrial group in Nigeria including Dangote Sugar Refinery, Dangote Cement, and Dangote Flour.

In July 2012, Dangote approached the Nigerian Ports Authorities to lease an abandoned piece of land at the Apapa Port, which was approved. He later built facilities for his flour company there. In the 1990s, he approached the Central Bank of Nigeria with the idea that it would be cheaper for the bank to allow his transport company to manage their fleet of staff buses, a proposal which was also approved.

In Nigeria today, Dangote Group with its dominance in the sugar market and refinery business is the main supplier (70% of the market) to the country's soft drinks companies, breweries and confectioners. It is the largest refinery in Africa and the third largest in the world, producing 800,000 tonnes of sugar annually. Dangote

Group owns salt factories and flour mills and is a major importer of rice, fish, pasta, cement and fertilizer. The company exports cotton, cashew nuts, cocoa, sesame seed and ginger to several countries. It also has major investments in real estate, banking, transport, textiles and oil and gas. The company employs over 11,000 people and is the largest industrial conglomerate in West Africa.

Dangote has diversified into telecommunications and has started building 14,000 kilometers of fiber optic cables to supply the whole of Nigeria. As a result, Dangote was honored in January 2009 as the leading provider of employment in the Nigerian construction industry.

He said, *"Let me tell you this and I want to really emphasize it...nothing is going to help Nigeria like Nigerians bringing back their money. If you give me $5 billion today, I will invest everything here in Nigeria. Let us put our heads together and work."* Such is the spirit of a man who truly understands Nigeria.

Dangote was named as the Forbes Africa Person of the Year 2014. The other nominees for the award were South Africa's Public Protector, Thuli Madonsela, Nigerian author, Chimamanda Ngozi Adichie, Director-General of the Securities and Exchange Commission, (SEC), Arunma Oteh, and President of the African Development Bank, Donald Kaberuka. In 2013, Alhaji Dangote and six other prominent Nigerians were conferred Honorary Citizenship of Arkansas State by Governor Mike Beebe who also proclaimed May 30 of every year as Nigeria Day in the US.

Dangote played a prominent role in the funding of Olusegun Obasanjo's re-election bid in 2003, to which he gave over N200 million (US$1M). He contributed N50 million (US$0.25M) to the National Mosque under the aegis of "Friends of Obasanjo and Atiku". He contributed N200 million to the Presidential Library.

On 23 May 2010, Britain's Daily Mirror reported that Dangote was interested in buying a 16 percent stake in Premiership side Arsenal belonging to Lady Nina Bracewell-Smith. Dangote later denied these rumors.

On 14 November 2011, Dangote was awarded Nigeria's second highest honour, the Grand Commander of the Order of the Niger (GCON) by the President, Goodluck Jonathan.

Dangote reportedly added $9.2 billion to his personal wealth in 2013, according to the Bloomberg Index, now making him the 30th richest person in the world, in addition to being the richest person in Africa.

In 2014, the Nigerian government said Dangote had donated 150 million Naira (US$750,000) to halt the spread of ebola.

In May 2015, Dangote expressed interest in purchasing the English football team Arsenal as widely reported by several news outlets including Wikipedia.

Dangote: a Man of Philanthropy and Sponsorship

Like we said earlier, Aliko Dangote is the richest person in Africa and is also one of the top 50 richest people in the world. He is also well-known for his generosity and for being humble about his kindness. Dangote made a public statement that he will only give some of his money to charity and not all. With donations of as much as US$185 million over the space of two years, 'some' of his money is clearly a substantial amount. The reason behind Dangote's generosity is claimed to be his belief that Africans should be helping Africa and other Africans.

Aliko Dangote started the Dangote Foundation in 1997. His aim was to start a charity that would act as a vehicle for his philanthropic deeds and corporate social responsibility actions. Through his efforts and with a generous endowment of US$1.25 billion, the foundation evolved into being the biggest private foundation in sub-Saharan Africa.

One of Aliko Dangote's biggest philanthropic achievements was when he worked with the Bill and Melinda Gates Foundation in 2013 on a project in Northern Nigeria. The aim of the project was to drastically reduce polio, and to improve immunization routines in the area. As a direct result of the initiative there were no new cases of polio between 2014 and 2016 when a few new cases were found.

Other major donations by Aliko Dangote include:

Developing the Dangote Academy with the aim of developing manpower in various sectors. The academy is worth around US$6 million.

Spending a further US$6 million on rehabilitating several universities in Nigeria.

Making a US$15.4 million donation in aid of cushioning the effects of floods that ravaged Nigeria. A further US$2.8 million was donated as relief aid for flood victims in the same year.

Donating US$3.3 million and relief items to the value of nearly US$250,000 to victims of a communal clash during insurgency.

In addition to his generous help to Nigerians, Aliko Dangote is also involved with helping other countries. Notable donations include:

Donating US$2 million to victims of floods in Pakistan.

Donating US$500,000 to victims of an explosion in the DRC.

Donating US$740,500 to battle the devastation of famine in Niger.

Extraordinary Feats by a Single Nigerian

Most people know the name Aliko Dangote, but not too many people know that the best has not yet been heard about Dangote. This man is a visionary extraordinaire. He plans to glorify Nigeria and put her on the world stage in grand style.

Dangote is poised to make his Nigerian based company the number one producers of cement in the world.

Dangote Cement is a fully integrated cement company and has projects and operations in Nigeria and 14 other African countries; Dangote Cement's current total production capacity in Nigeria from its three existing cement plants (Obajana 10.25MMTPA, Ibese 6.0MMTPA and Gboko 4.0MMTPA) is 20.25MMTPA.

The Obajana Cement Plant (OCP) located in Kogi State is reputed to be one of the single largest cement plants in the world with a combined capacity of 10.25MMTPA.

A fourth line which add 3.0MMTPA to the existing capacity will bring the total capacity of Obajana to 13.25MMTPA by 2015.

Dangote Cement is also the biggest quoted company in West Africa and the only Nigerian company on the Forbes Global 2000 Companies.

What a man. What a Nigerian. Such is the Nigerian spirit I have emphasized all along in this book. This is what Nigerians are capable of. I have every reasonable proof to announce to you and tell the whole wide world that Nigeria can indeed become the greatest country in the world.

I have come to personally admire Dangote for his efforts within Nigeria. Not just his efforts, but his vision for the country. Dangote has proven time and again, that he is a different form of elite.

Why Dangote is Losing Sleep

Dangote has revealed that the success or failure of any of his businesses does not bother him or make him lose sleep like the rate of unemployed Nigerian youths. In other words, the rate of unemployed youths in Nigeria is the principal reason why he is losing sleep as a Nigerian. Can you now X-ray this man's heart?

Dangote disclosed this in Lagos, Nigeria in May 2017.

He revealed that unemployment gives him sleepless nights, as he posited that it's the collective responsibility of both the government and entrepreneurs to create jobs for the teeming Nigerian youths as a way of solving the restiveness and agitations that the nation is experiencing from different geopolitical zones.

According to him, population growth is not abating as population and poverty go together especially in the northern part of the country where limitless procreation is recorded.

Dangote also harped on diversification as the major solution to the unemployment challenges the nation is facing, submitting sadly though, that successive governments had always paid lip service to job creation and diversification.

He said: "*Since 1978, when I came to Lagos, government has been talking about diversification of the economy which has not happened up till now. It is also sad that nobody is challenging anybody about how many jobs he or she has created.*

In reality though, it is not solely government duty to provide jobs. It is also the duty of entrepreneurs, but government at all levels must provide the enabling environment. When there is no jobs, people get frustrated, and I can tell you that the Boko Haram insurgency is a product of frustration. The way to go is diversification. Nigeria should diversify its economy, and take crude oil as icing on the cake."

If we have such a national treasure in Dangote, why is he not allowed to spearhead the diversification of our economy? Why is he not given the challenge and saddled with the responsibility of getting our teeming youths off the street. If a man among us who has the means and the proven results and also has the vision of solving our unemployment problems, I see no reason why such a man is not supported to solve and eradicate this problem.

Youth unemployment today in Nigeria stands at 25.20 % which is a disaster for any developing country. As you already know, unemployment and crime cannot be divorced from each other. Youth unemployment is the basis of Bokoharam, militancy, kidnapping, armed robbery, ritual killing and many of such likes.

This means that if we solve the problem of youth unemployment just as Dangote has opined, we would have effectively tackled the problem of security too. It is like the adage of using a stone to kill two birds. What a way to go. This is definitely a solid advice that must be followed.

Our priority right now therefore must be tackling youth employment as Dangote has advised. There are only a few people as qualified for the job as Dangote. Dangote should be put on the chair and saddled with the responsibility of building this as his own legacy. He would be forever remembered for taking jobless youths off the street and solving the problems of crime. He would be remembered for standing out of political office yet revolutionizing our nation. He should be given every resource needed and given quotas and targets to meet. He should become more celebrated as a national hero.

Nigeria should build her economy around such men, Dangote must be given targets. His assignment must be to raise other billionaires and men like himself. He must groom billionaires and other of such men. That way we are going to teach the world. That way we are going to become the greatest country in the world.

Surely, Dangote can produce at least one hundred billionaires using same system that has produced him. Surely, he can empower, mentor and show others the way like himself. Nigeria is great already having the richest black man on the earth as her son.

Dear friends, I so much believe in Nigeria. My reasons are not just because of emotions and sentiments. I mean, my believe is not because I come from Nigeria myself. Believe me I have traveled the world and I can tell you for a fact, there are no people like Nigerians. This is not about pride or arrogance, this is raw facts out of my interactions with people from almost every nation on earth. That is why nobody would make me keep quiet until we address and fix our vices as a nation. Because I want to see the full potential of Nigeria realized in my generation.

Not only his Dangote a fulfilled son of the soil, not only is Nigeria having the richest black man in the world as a citizen, the richest black woman in the world as well is a Nigerian. Wow! It is almost unbelievable but it is the truth. You have got to meet this woman of exceptional qualities and character, you have got to meet Mrs. Folorunso Alakija.

Folorunso Alakija: a Woman of Substance

Folorunso Alakija is a Nigerian businesswoman, one of the richest African women and also one of the richest black women in the world. In 2014 she unseated Oprah Winfrey as the richest black woman in the world.

She is a business tycoon involved in the fashion, oil and printing industries. She is the group managing director of The Rose of Sharon Group which consists of The Rose of Sharon Prints & Promotions Limited and Digital Reality Prints Limited and the executive vice-chairman of Famfa Oil Limited. Alakija is ranked by Forbes as the richest woman in Nigeria with an estimated net worth of $2.1 billion.

As of 2015, she is listed as the second most powerful woman in Africa after Ngozi Okonjo-Iweala (also a Nigerian) and the 87th most powerful woman in the world by Forbes.

Folorunsho was born in 1951 to the family of Chief L. A. Ogbara in Ikorodu, Lagos State. At age seven, she travelled to the United Kingdom to begin a four-year primary education at Dinorben School for Girls in Hafodunos Hall in Llangernyw, Wales. After returning to Nigeria, she attended Muslim High School Sagamu Ogun State, Nigeria. Afterwards, she returned abroad for her secretarial studies at Pitman's Central College, London. She also studied fashion design at the American College, London and the Central School of Fashion.

Folorunsho started her career in 1974 as an executive secretary at Sijuade Enterprises, Lagos, Nigeria. She moved on to the former First National Bank of Chicago, now FinBank now acquired by FCMB (First City Monument Bank) where she worked for some years before establishing a tailoring company called Supreme Stitches. It rose to prominence and fame within a few years, and as Rose of Sharon House of Fashion, became a household name. As national president and lifelong trustee of the Fashion Designers Association of Nigeria (FADAN), she left an indelible mark, promoting Nigerian culture through fashion and style.

In May 1993, Folorunsho applied for the allocation of an oil prospecting license (OPL). The license to explore for oil on a 617,000-acre block - now referred to as OPL 216 - was granted to Alakija's company, Famfa Limited. The block is located approximately 220 miles south east of Lagos and 70 miles offshore of Nigeria in the Agbami Field of the central Niger Delta.

In September 1996, she entered into a joint venture agreement with Star Deep Water Petroleum Limited (a wholly owned subsidiary of Texaco) and appointed the company as a technical adviser for the exploration of the license, transferring 40 percent of her 100 percent stake to Star Deep. Subsequently, Star Deep sold off 8 percent of its stake in OPL 216 to Petrobras, a Brazilian company.

On 9 March 2016 she became the first female Chancellor (Osun State University) in Nigeria.

As of 2014, she is listed as the 96th most powerful woman in the world by Forbes. In May 2015 two Nigerian women, Finance Minister Ngozi Okonjo-Iweala and Alakija were listed among the world's 100 most powerful women according to Forbes. Alakija was 87th on the list.

Folorunsho has a foundation called the Rose of Sharon Foundation that helps widows and orphans by empowering them through scholarships and business grants. Her company is also a major sponsor of the Agbami medical and engineering scholarship scheme, one of the most reliable scholarship scheme in Nigeria with over a thousand people yearly as beneficiaries. Mrs Alakija is a fervent supporter of education in Nigeria; for example in 2014 she donated a substantial amount of money to Ibrahim Badamasi Babangida University Lapai, the Niger State University. The money was used to complete the construction of a 350 Seat Lecture Theater, which was named after her.

On 1 July 2013, the federal government of Nigeria inaugurated the National Heritage Council and Endowment for the Arts and appointed Alakija as vice-chairman of the body.

She serves as the Chief Matron of Africa's Young Entrepreneurs.

Folorunsho Alakija has gotten it right understanding that the purpose of her wealth is to raise others. Like Dangote she is committed to the course of the underprivileged within and outside Nigeria.

Alakija's achievements is a clarion call to every woman in Nigeria. This can only mean that Nigerian women are not left out in the scheme of things.

Also, Nigeria stands to benefit so much from the philanthropic efforts of Mrs Alakija. Her foundation should be strengthened to help a lot of underprivileged Nigerians who for one reason or the other are in financial holes at the moment.

In another book of mine titled, "**ROLE OF THE ELITE IN NATIONAL TRANSFORMATION**", I have outlined how the Elite especially through Philanthropic efforts can actually transform a nation.

What gladdens my heart is that we have certain Nigerians already committed to this noble course. In fact, Nigerian philanthropists like Dangote and Alakija are some of the biggest philanthropists in the whole of Africa and rank also very highly in the world.

Other Nigerians who are so committed to wiping off tears the face of the poor masses include Jim Ovia, Tony Elumelu, Theophilus danjuma and Arthur Eze. Permit me to give you a glimpse of what these noble Nigerians are doing to make Nigeria the greatest country on earth. It will surely challenge every reader of this book.

Most Generous African Philanthropists

- **TONY ELUMELU**

Perhaps there are only a few men changing the face of Nigeria today like Tony Elumelu.

Tony Onyemaechi Elumelu (born 22 March 1963) is a Nigerian economist, entrepreneur, and philanthropist. He is the Chairman of Heirs Holdings, the United Bank for Africa, Transcorp and founder of The Tony Elumelu Foundation. Elumelu holds the Nigerian national honours, the Commander of the Order of the Niger (CON) and Member of the Order of the Federal Republic (MFR). He was recognised as one of "**Africa's 20 Most Powerful People in 2012**" by Forbes magazine.

Following his retirement from United Bank for Africa in July 2010, Elumelu founded The Tony Elumelu Foundation. His stated objective was to "prove that the African private sector can itself be the primary generator of economic development." The Foundation is charged with the mission of driving Africa's economic development by enhancing the competitiveness of the African private sector. As a premier pan-African-focused not-for-profit institution, the Tony Elumelu Foundation is dedicated to the promotion and celebration of entrepreneurship and excellence in business leadership across the continent, with initiatives such as The Tony Elumelu Entrepreneurship Program (TEEP).

TEF's activities revolve around:

1. Developing the next generation of business leaders for Africa

2. Building the networks and developing the framework for enhancing the competitiveness of African economies

3. Identifying impact investing opportunities.

4. Research work aimed at developing an enabling environment for African entrepreneurs

The Foundation has set itself apart from grant-making by operationalizing various integrated programs to support entrepreneurship in Africa and enhancing the competitiveness of the African private sector. TEF has built a reputation for successfully implementing diverse programs to achieve this, including:

- Promoting entrepreneurship e.g. Elumelu Professionals' Program (EPP), Nigeria 50, Impact investments, grant to CCHub, and recently its flagship - the TEEP;
- Enhancing competitiveness e.g. African Exchange (AFEX), National Competitiveness Council of Nigeria (NCCN), Blair-Elumelu Fellows Program;
- Selective grant making to other bodies pursuing aligned and strategic causes e.g. Tony Blair African Governance Initiative, Kofi Annan Foundation, John Kuffour Foundation, One Org, Rothschild Foundation;
- Policy development, research and advocacy through the Africapitalism Institute
- Leadership development and recognition of excellence e.g. The Tony & Awele Elumelu Prize (TAEP), The Fellows program

- Reports on the African entrepreneurial ecosystem, based on data collected from its 20,000+ pan-African network, resulting in two comprehensive reports, Unleashing Africa's Entrepreneurs and Unleashing Africa's Agricultural Entrepreneurs

Activities of Tony Elumelu Foundation

The Tony Elumelu Entrepreneurship Program (TEEP): A decade-long $100m initiative designed to give training, mentorship and seed capital to 10,000 entrepreneurs with start-up business ideas they want to execute in Africa.

The Mtanga Farms Investment: The Foundation's inaugural impact investment was in Mtanga Fars Limited, a mixed arable farming business operating in the Southern Tanzanian Highlands.

The Elumelu Legacy Prize: An award established by Tony O. and Dr. Awele Elumelu to recognize homegrown academic excellence in subject areas representing their career paths and fields of academic study. The awards are given to the overall best graduating students and best performing students in Economics, Business Administration, and Medicine within top tertiary institutions across Nigeria's six geopolitical zones. It is also given to recipients who have excelled in training programs from the Chartered Institute of Bankers of Nigeria. The annual Prize was designed to promote academic excellence and inspire the next generation of Nigerian leaders.

The Elumelu Professionals Program (EPP) recruits experienced professionals graduating from prestigious Masters in Business Administration and Masters in

Public Administration (or Public Policy) programs to work in SME companies and public sector agencies. The recruits work on specific strategic projects over the course of a 10-week placement. Since 2011, the Foundation has placed over 85 professionals in more than 40 companies across seven countries in Africa.

The Blair Elumelu Fellowship Program (BEFP) is a partnership between former British Prime Minister Tony Blair's Africa Governance Initiative and TEF. It is scheduled to run for three years. Tony Blair's office has hailed it as *"bringing together the best of innovative European government delivery models with the best of African private sector acumen and execution."*

The Global Impact Investing Network (GIIN) is a not-for-profit organization dedicated to increasing the effectiveness of impact investing. TEF is dedicated to impact investing and is a member of the GIIN Investor Council.

The Foundation's focus on research will see it deliver white papers on different topics in 2012. Their founder, Tony O. Elumelu, contributed to the Nigerian Leadership Initiative's white paper in 2011. The GIIN published a case study in November 2011 on the Foundation's investment in Mtanga Farms.

The Africapitalism Institute also released a comprehensive report on the entrepreneurial ecosystem in Africa, analyzing challenges facing African entrepreneurs and their proposed solutions. Titled Unleashing Africa's Entrepreneurs: Improving the Enabling Environment for Start-ups, it was first released to the public at a world-press conference on the sidelines of the 6th Global Entrepreneurship Summit in Nairobi, Kenya on

25 July 2015. The data used was based on original research leveraging the Foundation's pan-African network of over 20,000 early stage African businesses.

A leading light in African philanthropy, TEF has relationships with several other organizations around the world.

This is the power of a one man, this is what a man is doing to make Nigeria the greatest country in the world. The role of the elite and the privileged cannot be overemphasized in nation building. Kudos can only be given to the visionary Tony Elumelu. In fact, it is a privilege that we still have such a man with us today. He can only be encouraged to do more with his visionary strides.

There is no doubt that within a few years, Tony Elumelu would have totally changed the face of leadership not just in Nigeria, but indeed the rest of Africa.

- **JIM OVIA**

Jim Ovia is a veteran banker with more than three decades of experience in the industry. He is the founder of Zenith Bank in Nigeria where he worked for over 20 years as Chief Executive Officer and Group Managing Director. His leadership at the bank positioned Zenith as one of the most profitable, largest and most respected banks on the African continent. Zenith was founded by Ovia in 1990 and is licensed as a commercial bank. It has several subsidiaries including: Zenith Pension Custodian, Zenith Insurance, Zenith Bank Ghana, Zenith Bank UK, CyberSpace Networks and Zenith Trust Company. Ovia is responsible for introducing a range of innovations and technological developments in the banking industry in Nigeria that not only brought great success to Zenith, but also created a major industry-wide shift.

The Jim Ovia Foundation was launched with the aim of investing in the unlimited potential of the youths of Nigeria - and using this investment as a key to the social and economic growth of the nation. The foundation hopes to improve the standard of living in Nigerian society by increasing the efficiency in which people are operating. The long-term goal of the foundation is to use education and Information and Communication Technology (ICT) to enable the young people of Nigeria to be equipped to contribute to, and gain from the global economy. The foundation also aims to bring ICT into the school curriculum as an additional science, and hopes to foster an ICT literate society.

Supported causes include

Graduates of secondary schools, university students and ICT entrepreneurs who are eligible are invited to apply for:

- Educational scholarships
- ICT
- Grants/Award Programs

The Jim Ovia Scholarship

Founded and funded in 1998, the scholarship is available to 100 outstanding young Nigerians every year for funding undergraduate studies. Tuition and a maintenance allowance are covered by the scholarship. As in October 2010 ₦100 million (Nigerian Naira) had already been invested in the program. Scholarships are provided on the basis of intellectual ability, leadership qualities and the desire to become a valuable member of society.

The Jim Ovia ICT Entrepreneurs Program

The aim of the Jim Ovia ICT Entrepreneurs Program is to empower up-and-coming young ICT entrepreneurs to explore the African market. The program aims to nurture these entrepreneurs over a period of one year so that they may achieve their full potential. A hackathon is hosted by the program where between five and ten innovative ideas and 50 entrepreneurs are selected for funding every year. The entrepreneurs are given the necessary training and mentorship to achieve their goals.

Empower Youth Program

According to studies early intervention in the education of underprivileged youths can seriously affect the outcome of their lives in terms of social welfare, crime and graduation rates. The Empower YOUth Program is an initiative that aims to familiarize youths aged between six and 10 to become familiar with the digital age through ICT. The twelve week boot-camp program equips youths with ICT skills that will help them gain future access to the tech economy.

Foundation's History

The Jim Ovia Foundation was founded by Jim Ovia in August 2003 as a non-profit organisation with the aim of fostering social and educational upliftment to underserved young Nigerians and to bring ICT empowerment initiatives to Nigeria. To date the foundation has helped over 1,500 students and ICT entrepreneurs with educational and entrepreneurial grants. The foundation has spent more than ₦100 million (Nigerian Naira) on two of its nationally renowned initiatives: the Jim Ovia ICT Entrepreneurs Program and the Jim Ovia Scholarship. The beneficiaries of the foundation excel both academically and in community service and generally overcome tremendous challenges to pursue their dreams.

Jim Ovia is a great Nigerian who believes the potential of the Nigerian Project. So does another Nigerian Philanthropist and one of the biggest givers in Africa today to humanity, Arthur Eze.

- **ARTHUR EZE**

In a fine article written by Odimegwu Onwumere detailing the philanthropic efforts of Chief Arthur, he described Chief Arthur as an unusual man.

Nigerian oil tycoon, Prince Arthur Eze who embodies so many qualities of what a Prince represents - he is strapping, independent, father, politician, philanthropist, dynamic and Chairman of Atlas Oranto Petroleum.

There is a saying that philanthropy is a ministry and not a geographical term. Philanthropy flows from Prince Eze's loving heart, not actually from his rich bank accounts and business empires.

Prince Eze's act is in appraisal with a statement by Mahatma Gandhi, suggesting that the simplest acts of kindness are by far more powerful than a thousand heads bowing in prayer. Nevertheless, Prince Eze is not your everyday noisemaker, but he says his mind where necessary without fear or favour and donates unpredictably to both the rich and indigent without singing his praise, without deafening anybody's ear for cheap publicity. In the words of sages: A charitable man is like an apple tree - he gives his fruit and is silent; the philanthropist is like the hen. This epitomizes the attributes of Prince Arthur Eze.

It was revealed that the word philanthropy is in connection with the Greek Language meaning 'love for mankind.' Prince Eze is one man who has decided to walk in the light of love, for mankind, for many to see him in the court of openness, than in the court of destructive selfishness. Many financially opulent Nigerians are found in the later; they are squirrels, magpies, stashers. They hardly give out! But Prince Eze has been carving his name on hearts, while others do on tombstones.

Prince Eze is living a legacy into the minds of many and the stories they share about him are immeasurable. The billionaire businessman that owns several producing and non-producing oil and gas assets across Nigeria, Liberia, Equatorial Guinea and the Gambia, is known for giving, for easing another's heartache. In the recent past, a rating by Forbes suggested that Prince Eze donated $6.3 million (N1 billion) to flood relief efforts in Nigeria, apart from the donations he made to universities. The world believes that the most valued and consecrated moments of Prince Eze's lives are those filled with the spirit of giving. One Joseph B. Wirthlin as if talking to Prince Eze, said that the greater the measure of our love, the greater is our joy. In the end, the development of such love is the true measure of success in life.

Just in June 2015, Prince Eze put a smile on the lips of members of the Association of People Living with Sickle Cell Disorder (APLSCD), by donating the sum of N5 million lifeline for a Sickle cell standard clinic at Ukpo, Dunukofia Council Area of Anambra State, with expectation that the clinic would be commissioned on the World Sickle Cell Day by June 18, 2016. Prine Eze had also donated 1.8 billion naira ($12 million) to a Nigerian Church charity, St. Stephen's Anglican Deanery and Youth Development Centre, for youth development. The man made the donation in Lagos at the church's fund raising chaired by the then President Goodluck Jonathan, whose hometown church was the recipient of the funds.

Prince Eze has a heart reaching down and lifting people up. In July 2014, Governor Willie Obiano of Anambra State, accompanied by his deputy, Dr. Nkem Okeke and the then National Chairman of APGA, Sir Victor Umeh, paid Prince Eze a courtesy call at his splendid home of Ukpo in Dunukofia Kingdom of Anambra State.

In that courtesy call, Prince Eze donated the sum of $1m for the program in the state to crackdown on criminals. He also assured the sum of one billion naira to sustain the governor's agricultural program.

Making the donation in his palatial home of Ukpo in Dunukofia Kingdom of Anambra State, when the governor, accompanied by his deputy, Dr. Nkem Okeke and the National Chairman of APGA, Sir Victor Umeh, paid him a courtesy call, Prince Eze who is a famous philanthropist and a chieftain of the People's Democratic Party, explained that the gesture was intended to encourage Governor Obiano's efforts to make Anambra State a livable and business-friendly environment for all.

Apart from making donations in monetary aspect, Prince Eze donates his time for peace against party line. He's of the belief that nothing can bring a division between him and his home state, not even politics. The philanthropist Prince Eze who is a stakeholder in the Peoples Democratic Party while Obiano is of the APGA sees nothing wrong in working in synergy to support the government by any positive means necessary, thereby shaving the animosity that is always in party line. He was of the gesture that Governor Obiano has shown gargantuan wisdom in bringing the issue of security first in his menu.

Following the statement by one G.K. Chesterton, saying that *"the whole modern world has divided itself into Conservatives and Progressives; the business of Progressives is to go on making mistakes; the business of Conservatives is to prevent mistakes from being corrected"*, it is not easy to say where Prince Eze belongs in the two. This is why he is simply referred to as a philanthropist; because he loathes any authority that makes colossal mistake or that prevents the correction of mistakes. To buttress this point, he cried out in July 2015, that one year after, Nigerian billionaires and government were yet to redeem to victims of Boko Haram bomb attacks vows, one year after the lavish fund-raiser in Abuja.

Checks revealed that the government fund-raiser which held on July 31, scraped in N54.7 billion in pledged donations from the federal and state governments, and the private sector. While the government was said to have donated N20 billion, key oil and gas operators gave N17 billion, banking sector offered N15 billion; investor Tony Elumelu gave N2.5 billion; and former defense minister, T.Y. Danjuma promised N1.6billion; the 36 states and the FCT gave N3.7billion; Arthur Eze and Mohammed Indimi gave N800million each; Folorunsho Alakija, Dahiru Mangal, Abdul Samad Rabiu, N500million each; Aliko Dangote, Zenith bank chief, Jim Ovia, Wale Tinubu, Mike Adenuga, donated N1billion each; making the donated sum exceed the government's target by N8 billion.

However, Prince Arthur Eze was in June 2015 deemed the eighth richest person in Africa with a net worth of more than $5.8 billion.

Nigeria is blessed with illustrious sons and daughters whose synergy and collaboration can bring Nigeria out of the woods within the shortest possible time.

Every one of us Must be Involved in Nation Building

This chapter has highlighted and praised some of Nigeria's finest and daughters and has thrown a challenge to the elite, the government and every reader of this book to awake and raise Nigeria from the state in which we are to become the giant of not just Africa, but the giant of the world. It is our collective responsibility, and we all must take up the challenge.

Finally, Professor Isa Hussaini of Faculty of Pharmacy University of Maiduguri wrote this beautiful lines and I have decided to include it in this book:

The blame for what Nigeria has become falls on you and me. Not Buhari, not Jonathan, not Obasanjo and definitely not Abacha.

Our wickedness stinks to the heavens as we go about our daily lives, pulling down everyone and everything to become rich. We import substandard products, fake drugs and expired baby food unfit for human consumption and we have the nerve to complain about leadership?

We even steal from widows, orphans, and refugees. We take their food and sell it for profit. No conscience. Nothing is sacred. No one is spared. We build substandard roads, schools, houses, hospitals, all for profit at the expense of human life;an invaluable item which all our profit and contract sum cannot buy.

One would think this behavior is reserved for urchins but it would surprise you that this is the character of many decent looking people who appear to be normal but are not any better than Boko Haram members. They are church members, Muslims, husbands, wives and sadly youths.

We pervert justice and pretend we do not know right from wrong just to serve our selfish interests. Slave traders pale in comparison to what we do to ourselves. We are wickedness personified. So much hatred flows in our blood and we transfer it to our children. It's evident in what we say and do.

We have fasting and prayer sessions all year long, night vigils and deliverance when the actual problem is us. We simply cannot learn to love others. It is me, me, me. That is all that ever matters. It is sickening. Anyone who cannot love has no business in politics, Government and in Nigeria. Until we understand this, we will continue on this path of destruction.

I can Change, You can Change, They can Change and We can Change by becoming this message....Change starts with Me.

NUGGETS

- Dangote should be put on the chair and saddled with the responsibility of eradicating youth unemployment as his personal legacy.
- Nigerian Philanthropists like Dangote and Alakija are some of the biggest philanthropists in the whole of Africa and rank also very highly in the world.
- Tony Elumelu can within a few years change the face of leadership not just in Nigeria, but indeed the rest of Africa.
- *"The simplest acts of kindness are by far more powerful than a thousand heads bowing in prayer".* ***Gandhi.***
- Nigeria is blessed with illustrious sons and daughters whose synergy and collaboration can bring Nigeria out of the woods within the shortest possible time
- It is our collective responsibility to make Nigeria the greatest country in the world, and we all must take up the challenge.
- The blame for what Nigeria has become falls on you and me.
- Change starts with me, change starts with you.

CHAPTER EIGHT

HOW TO BUILD NIGERIA'S ECONOMY

No doubt, it has been a very interesting discussion so far in this book. Without a shadow of doubt, Nigerians can hold their head up high again.

We have looked at various things that has made Nigeria an enviable nation and the rising sun of the world.

It is rather unfortunate though that when you speak with many Nigerians, especially those who live and reside within the borders of Nigeria, they tend not to see Nigeria as a great nation and a nation which can become the greatest country in the world if it lives out its full potential. Many people's gaze are simply fixed on every negative thing happening within Nigeria oblivious of the fact that so much greatness also happen here too. In fact, the kind of greatness that Nigerians achieve both within and outside Nigeria is such that the world bows to. One of such is what will be the focus of our discussion in this book.

There is no reason not to believe that Nigeria will be great again. There is no reason why Nigeria should not return to the lead of the world.

Unusual Feats

Apart from showing you exceptional Nigerians in the last chapter, who actually form a pool that Nigeria can draw from any time, I want to show you classic examples of how Nigeria has actually taken the world by storm, broken unusual records and indeed has demonstrated that it is capable of becoming the greatest country in the world.

After the successful democratic elections in Nigeria in 2003, the key priority for the Obasanjo-led administration was to institute - and follow through with - far-reaching, multi-faceted reforms in all sectors of the economy. According to experts, during Obasanjo's first term (1999-2003), the administration had been unable to drive through any large-scale reforms in the major sectors of the economy successfully due to the institutional challenges created by the previous sixteen years of military rule.

By 2003, President Obasanjo was able to assemble a cohesive team of Western-trained economists, some of them with experience in multilateral institutions such as the World Bank, in order to develop an economic blueprint, a reform strategy, and a more concerted strategic approach to reform. These reforms were expected to cover decentralization and macroeconomic balance and efficiency, including the optimal use of increasing oil revenues in a federal state. Decentralization was the arrowhead of the reforms and involved decentralizing some hitherto protected industries, privatizing government holdings in business concerns, and strengthening the non-federal arms of government.

The impetus for the reforms was psychological, domestic and international.

First, President Obasanjo recalled the Nigerian economy, and its supporting physical infrastructure, as a functional state when he left power as a military ruler in 1979: in sharp contrast to the comatose system he encountered when he regained power as a civilian president twenty years later.

Second was Nigerians' domestic yearning for change after 16 years of military rule. Third was the clarion call for reforms by international investors, in particular the multilateral agencies and the US government, who insisted on comprehensive socio-economic reforms as a sine qua non for any large-scale investment in Nigeria and as a prerequisite for moral support of the new administration.

The economic reforms were comprehensive. They straddled seven main areas: the civil service; power; transport; the legal system; the ports; telecommunications; and financial services (mainly banking).

However, the political maneuvers of the idle rich, who had sponsored the various democratic campaigns, burdened the President with inept nominees to the cabinet and other executive positions in the federal government, limiting the success of his reforms during his first term in office.

By the end of the first term, it had become obvious that financial sector reforms, which were initially synonymous with banking, were most likely to have the greatest and quickest impact, at least in the short term. Inflation had reached 10% (increasing later to almost 14%), the GDP growth rate was still at a mere 3–4% (barely 1% ahead of the population growth rate) and official unemployment was worsening.

Inflation and unemployment had become the two albatrosses of the economy. Inflation, manifested in wildly fluctuating prices, created widespread uncertainty. Unemployment, on the other hand, created a large army of dependents, bred corruption and fed booming crime.

Battling inflation was the key priority. This required dealing with several factors, including the fiscal deficit, interest rates and the money supply.

In Nigeria, tackling interest rates alone would not have had sufficient impact on the money supply problem due to the large scale of black market money exchanges, money laundering, money trafficking, and a whole array of other economic crimes. The only solution, it seemed, was wholesale reform of the financial sector, in particular the notorious banking sector, which, uniquely, had been growing rapidly, at an average of 44 per cent per annum, in an economy which, for the most part, was gradually collapsing.

Using Experts to Transform the Economy

The key assumption was that reforming Nigeria's financial system would be a catalyst for economic growth – or at least reduce the leakages and economic sabotage for which the banking sector was notorious. Hence Obasanjo began the delicate Bank reform with

Prof. Charles Soludo at the helm as the central Bank Governor.

When Professor Charles Chukwumah Soludo became Governor of the Central Bank of Nigeria, CBN, the general perception was that another Mohammed Ali of Egypt and Emperor Menelik of Ethiopia or Henrique Cardoso of Brazil had come to reform the ailing economy. In his maiden address in 2004, Soludo announced a 13 point reforms program for the Nigerian Banks.

The primary objective of the reforms was to guarantee an efficient and sound financial system. There was need to reposition the banking system with a view to developing the requisite flexibility to support the economic development of the nation. The reforms sought to ensure a diversified, strong and reliable banking industry where there would be safety of depositors' money; so that banks can play active developmental roles in the Nigerian economy.

The key elements of the 13-point reform program of Central Bank include:

- Minimum capital base of N25billion with a deadline of 31st December, 2005
- Consolidation of banking institution through mergers and acquisition;
- Phased withdrawal of public sectors funds from banks, beginning from July 2004;
- Adoption of a risk-focused and rule based regulatory framework;
- Zero tolerance for weak corporate governance, misconduct and lack of transparency.
- Accelerated completion of the Electronic Finan-

cial Analysis Surveillance System (e-FASS).

- The establishment of an Asset Management Company.
- Promotion of the enforcement of dormant laws.
- Revision and updating of relevant laws.
- Closer collaboration with the EFCC and the establishment of the Financial Intelligence Unit.

Of all reforms agenda the issue of increasing stakeholders fund to N25 billion generated so much controversy especially among the stakeholders and the need to comply before 31st December 2005.

He assumed office as the CBN Chief and rolled out seemingly innovation action programs, the most prominent being the banking sector reforms, privatization of government enterprises and other IMF – inspired policies ostensibly designed to reposition the tottering economy. First he hurriedly closed down most banks by raising the liquidity ratio and in one fell swoop, 64 banks submarined. Secondly he advised ex-president Obasanjo to privatize most of the government owned enterprises.

By the end of December 2005, the entire system had been consolidated into 25 banks, and the licenses of 14 insolvent banks were revoked in January 2006. It was the first time in Nigeria that a major policy had been announced and clinically concluded on deadline.

"We also held the world record for achieving, for the first time, a consolidation of such magnitude without recourse to the public treasury – it cost the Nigerian Government nothing," says Soludo proudly. *"It sent a clear and unmistakable message to the rest of the banking sector that ours*

was a no-nonsense regime, and that the rules would be applied, no matter whose ox was gored."

Achieving Global Records Economically

Barely a year after the consolidation, 14 Nigerian banks were ranked among the top 1,000 in the world, and in 2008, two of them were in the top 300. The banks were now in a position to fund projects worth billions of dollars in oil and gas, manufacturing and infrastructure.

"It was a new dawn for the banking system," says Soludo. *"The public offers by the banks in order to recapitalize also revolutionized public awareness of the capital market. The sector boomed in subsequent years and rose to a capitalization of nearly $100b before the global financial crisis."*

Well, what began as reform projects in the banking sector yielded enormous long-term fruits asides the short term benefits that Nigerians enjoyed. You may not believe it but the facts are here. Nigeria is the rising star of the future world because of the PHENOMENAL GROWTH OF THE NIGERIAN BANKS.

Thirteen Nigerian banks have been listed among the Leading 1000 Global Banks as published by The Banker magazine of the Financial Times Group in its 2014 edition.

The Nigerian banks that made the ranking based on Tier-1 capital are Zenith Bank, Guaranty Trust Bank, First Bank, Access Bank, United Bank for Africa, Fidelity Bank and Ecobank Nigeria.

Others are Skye Bank, First City Monument Bank, Diamond Bank, Stanbic IBTC Holdings, Standard Chartered Bank Nigeria and Union Bank of Nigeria.

The report, which listed 13 Nigerian banks that made the ranking, underlines Nigeria's financial sector's leading position in Africa as no other African country has up to 13 banks in the Top 1000 World listing of banks.

According to the report, Zenith Bank ranked top in Nigeria at 293 in the world. Guaranty Trust is number 415 in the world. First Bank is number 424 in the world. Access Bank is number 532. United Bank for Africa ranked 539. And Fidelity ranked 622 position.

I don't have any doubt in my heart that with an increase in stability of our economic and political life, our banks could only rank higher and higher. The sky is the limit for the future of Nigeria and Africa as a whole.

Employing the Strategy that Works

Obasanjo's bank restructuring was absolutely phenomenal. It became the pathway to Nigeria's economic future and a solid blueprint for subsequent governments. Unfortunately, many political tenures after President Obasanjo failed to toll same line of aggressive economic development.

As things stand, why do we not employ the same strategy which has been proven and shown to work? Why don't we bring a lot more banks together, why don't we bring perhaps ten banks together to be among the top 10 in the world? Why don't we maximize the brain that we have and raise the bar? All the brightest minds

Nigeria has in large stock, especially a lot of them serving as consultants to the world bank can be brought together to achieve more. These brilliant minds include Ngozi Okonjo-Iweala, Oby Ezekwesili, Charles Soludo and the current Emir of Kano, Sanusi Lamido Sanusi.

Not many people, including Nigerians know that Nigeria's economic future remains optimistic. According to a recent survey by Business Insider, the country is projected to be among the 10 fastest economies in the world by 2020.

What this projection means is that Nigeria can conveniently strive to become the fastest developing economy in the world till it becomes the biggest economy in the world.

I guess you will be prouder of Nigeria if you know that Nigeria's economy is growing five times faster than the US.

Like I said earlier, the country is listed among the "Next Ten" economies, and is one of the fastest growing in the world with the International Monetary Fund projecting growth of 9 per cent in 2008 and 8.3 per cent in 2009. Of course, till date Nigeria has the biggest economy in the whole of Africa. A feat it achieved in 2016.

According to healthy Consultants, a reputable group of economic consultants, most people don't associate "West Africa" and "booming economy", but despite the global downturn, the region is home to some growth rates that would make Ronald Reagan blush. Right near the top of that list is Nigeria, that with an average growth rate of 8.1%, are experiencing more growth than the US (at 1.5%), the UK, Canada, Australia, Japan and the entire European Union… combined. I think Nigerians have every cause to be extremely proud. This sort of achievement is just rare and it is happening in Nigeria. Confidently we can say, Nigeria is becoming the greatest country in the world, Nigeria is the rising sun of the world.

Building our Economy Through Agriculture

A major way by which Nigeria is going to achieve her economic potential is through Agriculture.

Nigeria has the potential to be the key exporter of agricultural produce to the world. It has over 84 million hectares of arable land - larger than the size of turkey and a lot of the African countries.

According to Forbes, Agriculture is the future of Nigeria. Agriculture is a major means by which Nigeria can become the greatest country in the world.

In the 1960s, before it turned to oil, Nigeria was one of the most promising agricultural producers in the world. Between 1962 and 1968, export crops were the country's main foreign exchange earner. The country was number one globally in palm oil exports, well ahead of Malaysia and Indonesia, and exported 47 percent of all groundnuts, putting it ahead of the US and Argentina.

But its status as an agricultural powerhouse has declined, and steeply. While Nigeria once provided 18 percent of the global production of cocoa, second in the world in the 1960s, that figure is now down to 8 percent. And while the country produces 65 percent of tomatoes in West Africa, it is now the largest importer of tomato paste. While it gave Palm oil seedlings to Malaysia and

Indonesia to grow and cultivate, those countries are now larger producers of the oil palm than Nigeria.

Nigeria's former minister for agriculture, Akinwumi Adesina, once decried the country's deteriorating agriculture sector. *"Nigeria is known for nothing else than oil, and it is so sad, because we never used to have oil – all we used to have was agriculture,"* he says.

Nigeria's oil has come at the detriment of the agriculture sector, he claims, *"and that is why we had a rising poverty situation. We were having growth but without robust growth able to impact millions of people because it is not connecting to agriculture."*

That might explain why Nigeria's economic statistics are so puzzling. While the country has been posting high growth figures, and makes it into Goldman Sachs' 'Next 10' emerging markets group, absolute poverty is rising, with almost 100 million people living on less than a $1.25 a day. The National Bureau of Statistics says 60.9 percent of Nigerians in 2010 were living in absolute poverty, up from 54.7 percent in 2004.

But it is not just oil that has hollowed out the agriculture sector, with knock-on effects on poverty rates. Restrictive trade policies also had an effect, especially in the late 1970s and early 1980s. Tariff increases, a rise in import licenses and duties, and export bans and tariffs – as well as a centralization of marketing of agricultural produce through the formation of crop-specific commodity boards – all created a lumbering, inefficient private sector, as well as opening up many opportunities for corruption. Today, Nigeria has transitioned from being a self-sufficient country in food to being a net importer, spending $11bn on imports of rice, fish and sugar. *"It just makes absolutely no sense to me at all,"* says Mr Adesina. *"My job is to change that."*

The change needed, he says, requires a shift in mindset. *"We were not looking at agriculture through the right lens. We were looking at agriculture as a developmental activity, like a social sector in which you manage poor people in rural areas. But agriculture is not a social sector. Agriculture is a business. Seed is a business, fertilizer is a business, storage, value added, logistics and transport - it is all about business."*

Mr Adesina, who was awarded numerous continental awards for his achievements in Nigeria's agricultural sector, and later got voted as president of Africa's Development Bank changed the sector's image, putting it at the forefront of national development. *"Agriculture is the future of Nigeria. And agriculture that is modernized, that is productive, that is competitive. We must be a global player,"* he says.

Nigeria's respected former finance minister, Ngozi Okonjo-Iweala, speaks positively about Mr Adesina's in Nigeria's agricultural sector – especially in cleaning up the corrupt fertilizer industry. Now, rather than directly participating in the delivery system for fertilizer, the government leaves that to the private sector and only provides the subsidy. This change has tackled 40 years of corruption, and ended. A feat that won global recognition and accolades.

Changing the Status Quo

Nigeria is already on the right path now by seeking to add 20m metric tonnes to the domestic food supply each year and to create 3.5 million jobs through agriculture.

This is going to require from us more sophisticated thinking about the value addition of individual crops – cassava being but one example. We are the largest producer of cassava in the world, at 40m metric tonnes, but we must become the largest processor of cassava as well. We can focus on using cassava for starch, dry cassava chips for export to China, cassava flour to replace some of the wheat flour that we are importing. So we must embark on restructuring the space for the private sector to add value to every single thing.

Our big banks must start looking at the opportunities offered by agriculture – We need to root out corruption and improve efficiency in the system for effective utilization of allocation to agriculture.

The government must reduce the risk of agricultural lending by providing credit risk guarantees and brokerage services to buyers and sellers of agricultural commodities. The government should also, selectively, buy farm products on its own account to bring stability to markets. When we combine any of these solutions, no doubt, Nigeria is headed to become the greatest country in the world.

Rather than a heavy handed intervention in the sector, we must involve the banking sector in our agricultural reforms as well as investors. With banks, we will need not beg them to lend because they are taking care of their people's money, so by creating the value they need, they see the value and lend.

While banks have often had a high perceived risk of lending to agriculture, the terms can be competitive if the sector functions well. The government must work directly with the managing directors of banks.

If the sector's flaws – including inefficiencies and corruption – could be cleaned up. What we will show the banks and investors is that agriculture returns and benefits are as high and competitive a rate of return as other sectors if structured properly. But for banks to lend, we have to fix the agricultural value chain.

Finally, it is it is institutional reform - rather than simply heavier public spending - which can best unleash financing in the agricultural sector and cause it to become the greatest agricultural sector of any nation in the world. I do not think that throwing money at anything solves problems. It is all about policy reforms, creating incentives, getting the private sector in there, getting financial markets behind agriculture. Our goal must be to become an agriculturally industrialized economy. Nigeria should be like Brazil, as far as I am concerned.

Are you a Nigerian? Are you proud of your heritage? Have you seen now that there is absolutely wrong with Nigeria? Can you now see that Nigeria is truly destined for greatness? Now I know you will convincingly believe if I tell you that together, we can make Nigeria, the greatest country in the world, even economically.

NUGGETS

- There is no reason not to believe that Nigeria will be great again. There is no reason why Nigeria should not return to the lead of the world.
- The sky is the limit for the future of Nigeria and Africa as a whole.
- A major way by which Nigeria is going to achieve her economic potential is through Agriculture.
- Our big banks must start looking at the opportunities offered by agriculture – We need to root out corruption and improve efficiency in the system
- Nigeria is truly destined for greatness.

CHAPTER NINE

MAKING NIGERIA THE GREATEST COUNTRY IN THE WORLD

Wow! What a journey we have had in this book. What an incredible journey. If I read your mind well, there is no doubt that you are now convinced that truly Nigeria can become the greatest country in the world. We have seen examples of many ways that Nigeria is already setting pace for the world.

Nigeria as you have seen in this book is one of the most peculiar, distinct and enviable nations in the world. Let me reiterate at this point that soon enough, this country will be one which everyone desires to be in. Nigeria will be the place where the eyes of the world will be set. It will be the desire of nations. Through the many exploits of Nigerians in this book which can be duplicated in larger scales and amount, Nigeria will simply become an epitome of excellence, beauty and wonder.

Becoming the greatest nation on earth is simple and achievable. Through this book, you have seen many road maps which I already highlighted.

Becoming the greatest country in the world is our destiny, we are to lead the world. If we have to lead the world, we have to produce more men like those ones we have constantly read about in this book. This is our collective fate. We can lead the world in every sphere. That was why we had to see examples of men who are leading the world in every chapter of this book. However, there is one man you are yet to see. Who is this man?

In all humility, and finally, I am not going to allow anybody to forget about Pastor Sunday Adelaja. The only black man in the world that leads a congregation of mostly Caucasians in 50 countries. Below are some facts about Pastor Sunday's life and ministry.

Pastor Sunday is the pastor of the largest Evangelical Church in Europe with a population of 99.9% white Europeans in Kiev Ukraine.

His ministry has charity units that feed over 5000 people on a daily basis.

Through his ministry over 30 thousand people have been delivered from drug and alcohol addictions.

He helped raise over 200 millionaires in US dollars in his church, most of whom were former drug/ alcohol addicts and societal outcasts.

He has raised a global movement that is influencing over 70million people around the globe.

Branches of his church are in over 50 countries.

He has spoken in different nations of the world on National Transformation.

Pastor Sunday is one of the few, if not the only African, who has ever spoken in the US senate.

Pastor Sunday is one of the few African pastors who has spoken on the floor of the UN.

He has addressed the Japanese Members of parliament.

He has spoken in the Knesset to members of Israeli parliament. The list goes on and on.

His ministry has over 500 hundred government officials holding different government positions in Ukraine.

He has written and published over 300 books and recorded thousands of messages.

Well, Pastor Sunday had also been your author all along through this book's journey. I am Pastor Sunday.

Pastor Sunday's Mission to Nigeria

Many people have challenged me to come to Africa to contribute my quota. I have no doubt about it. I am coming sooner or later. Right now I am busy fighting the demons, forces of evil and principalities of Europe and Russia. But, in the meanwhile, I am also thinking about my beloved county Nigeria and mother Africa for which I am developing some grand plans and projects. By the grace of God, by the time I am privileged to come to Africa, everything I have achieved so far would dwarf compared to what I would be doing for the African continent by God's grace.

Now on a personal note, I would like to say that when I was growing up in Africa, I never saw anything special about myself that could distinguish me from the millions of kids in my nation. As a matter of fact, there are still so many millions of Sunday Adelajas wasting away in their villages and hamlets without any sort of recognition whatsoever.

I was destined to be in their number if not for divine grace. Whenever I visit Nigeria I see myself in all those young men. I see myself in those barefooted boys and girls running about the streets with protruding stomachs without shirts, hawking one product or the other for survival. That was me!

In fact, I still count it the biggest miracle of my life when a distant relative paid off my fifty naira WAEC fee (Final high school exams). Otherwise I was on my way out into the world without a high school certificate, because of fifty naira that my whole family could not come up with. Friends, believe me mine was not the only case. Cases like this abound in their millions all over Nigeria and Africa.

Many of them are wasted in the villages and farms of the continent. The Emeagwalis, the Adelajas, the Chimamandas, the Ogunlesis, the Dangotes, the Imafidons, the Okoyas etc. Imagine what awaits Nigeria when all our potential is harnessed towards the development of every Citizen, Nigeria, Africa and the world at large. Imagine what will happen to Nigeria when the genius in every child is unlocked.

Sunday Adelaja transcends Pastoring, I am fully committed to education. There is a grand design to start multiple Universities in my lifetime of which the University of Life has begun and is running adequately. I am committed to writing books and the ultimate development of the human mind. I am committed to humanity as a whole. I am committed to Nigeria in particular.

The Nigeria Transformation Project

My commitment has led me to create what is now called the Nigeria Transformation Project, a project that will reform Nigeria within the shortest time possible. The project is multi-faceted aimed at every sector of Nigeria including health, energy and power, education, welfare, economy, Agriculture, infrastructure and people empowerment. I have seen that developing a nation is not rocket science, as my antecedence as a foreigner in Ukraine proves. If I have been able to do many of what I have done in Ukraine as a foreigner, how much more my own land where I am a born son. The Nigeria Transformation project is here for good. Together we will build Nigeria and make it the greatest country in the world.

Now, remember that a few years ago, I was just one hopeless kid on the streets of Nigeria who could not even pay fees for my final high school exam. Someone paid that fee for me miraculously. If that fee was not paid, I'd probably still be farming in Idomila today.

My story strongly proves that every child has hope. Every child has a destiny him. Every child is a star. Every Nigerian child can become that instrument that will turn around to help us build the greatest country in the world. If Sunday Adelaja could be raised to become a transformation expert and a world changer, then every child can.

This places on us the need to believe in every Nigerian as a person that can lead the world, in spite of what condition and situation in which they currently are. There is a bigger responsibility for the elites of the society to play in this. I have discussed this in greater details in another book titled 'Role of the elite in national transformation'.

In closing this book, I must once again say that I HAVE NO DOUBT THAT NIGERIA WILL ONE DAY LEAD OUR WORLD!

Getting it Right

This book is called "**How to make Nigeria the greatest country in the world**". But in the same vein, it could easily be called: The Next World Super Power or When Africa Leads the World.

I see that many people who know me can't seem to understand the reason for my passion about Nigeria. I have seen the future of this country.

> Let others lead small lives, but not you. Let others argue over small things, but not you. Let others cry over small hurts, but not you. Let others leave their future in someone else's hands, but not you.
>
> Jim Rohn

Besides I have been privileged to compete in universities where we had students from 99 countries of the world and a Nigerian was leading the pack. This is not unusual as seen in the stories above. In over 60 countries of the world where I have been, Nigerians are always the head and not the tail, the first and not the last.

I remember in 2005 while in Seoul South Korea. Some South Koreans scientists told me they carried out an experiment, which showed that Nigerians have one of the 3 top IQ's in the world. As a matter of fact, a Nigerian whom we have already talked about Phillip Emeagwali is rated among the top 10 most intelligent people in the world. He is rated to have an Intelligent Quotient of 190. The most intelligent man in the world is Terrence Tao of China and has a verified IQ of 230

Everything points to the fact that Nigeria is the rising sun of the world.

Nigerians are resilient, hardworking, passionate, enterprising and aggressive even though most people tend to unfairly emphasize only the negative part of Nigerians, but there is much more to Nigerians than negative tendencies. I admit we are not without our demons, yet as said by Mario Andretti

> IF EVERYTHING IS UNDER CONTROL, YOU ARE NOT GOING FAST ENOUGH.
>
> MARIO ANDRETTI

Can you imagine, a country where there is NO functioning electricity 24 hours? What will begin to happen if all our citizens have a 100% electricity supply? If Nigerians could come top in all the above listed areas of life, without any basic amenities. Imagine then what will happen if they were to have all these things.

Friends, can you imagine what would happen if every Nigerian child, in every village is raised up in a sanitized environment, with good nutrition, libraries, water supply, transportation system, equal opportunities, access to money, education, good health facilities etc. We don't have much yet, still we are leading the world. What will happen if all the above mentioned facilities are in place?

We know the long list of our failures, despite all the things we lack as a nation, yet we perform. Now imagine what could have been. Today Nigeria's economy is ranked number 26 in the world.

> BUT MANY THAT ARE FIRST SHALL BE LAST; AND THE LAST SHALL BE FIRST.
>
> MATT 19:30

I am convinced that if we get just one thing right which is electricity. Our GDP growth will double from 6% yearly to 12% which will propel us to become one of the top 3 countries in the world in the next 20 years.

I believe in Nigeria, that is why I would not compromise nor refrain from speaking the whole truth and nothing but the truth. The truth that will be able to set us free from the shackles of our weaknesses and inadequacies and propel us into our glorious destiny.

NIGERIA: A UNIQUE NATION

In closing this book, let me bring back some of the words I started this book with. If you have ever had a trip to Nigeria or if you are a non-Nigerian reading this, can I ask you some questions? What struck you about Nigerians the most? Beyond the roads which currently are not in the best of shape and the menace on our streets, what else did you see? Was there anything that appealed to you specially?

As a Nigerian, what do you value most about your country? Beyond the political manipulations and the general state of things currently, beyond the hardship of the economy and other unpalatable stories, what else do you see and think? Do you perceive anything magnificent?

One thing you are not likely to miss even if you only get to spend a few minutes within the borders of the country is the spirit of Nigerians. What will fascinate you the most about Nigeria is her people. The greatest thing you are likely to get drawn to about Nigeria is the heart, the resilience, the creativity, the innovation, brilliance, genius, hospitality, tenacity, energy, competitiveness and optimistic spirit of Nigerians. I could write expansively on each of this points and how they are generously manifested in Nigerians. In many places, this has come to be known as the Nigerian spirit.

The Power of the Nigerian Spirit

As you have seen in every chapter of this book, especially the numerous examples I gave, the never-die Nigerian spirit is a force which seems to be well known and respected. It is present in our homes, in our communities, in our neighborhoods, in our schools, in our market places, in our offices and everywhere you go or find a Nigerian. With such force and domineering spirit, is why Nigerians rule in many fields of endeavors around the world.

Nigerians by nature are extremely competitive people. Nigerians are bold, fierce, resilient, confrontational and passionate. It is almost a taboo to find a Nigerian who is lazy or who does not want to win and lead the pack. No matter what nation you live in, if you have ever come across Nigerians, you cannot but agree with me.

Like I earlier wrote about, when I was in school almost thirty years ago, we had students from about ninety nine countries. What was shocking was that Nigerians were conveniently leading the rest of the students, the entire school and even the indigenous students. They led the school in a way and manner typically Nigerian and made it look as if leading was easy. When they were conveniently leading other students within the school, they had to begin to compete within themselves and among themselves to be the best. Needless to say, I was one of them.

That same fighting spirit is what you have all around the world today and everywhere you see a Nigerian. It is that spirit that wants to make a Nigerian win at any cost. When you find them as a community within another country, they are easily noticed. Within a time, they begin to take over everywhere, they simply dominate. This extra ordinary feat may bring them jealousy, hatred and hostility, but you cannot take that grace and ability from them. Indeed, Nigerians are very special people just like the Jews. Another group of people in the world who have and possess something similar to the traits and characteristic of Nigerians is the Jews.

Striking Similarities Between Jews and Nigerians

There are some very striking similarities between Nigerians and Jews. They have something very similar in spirit and attitude. There is something about the Jews, same with Nigerians that the rest of the world has not come to understand, including many Nigerians themselves. It seems though that the Jews understand their own peculiarity, hence are using same to dominate the world. When Nigeria also takes advantage of this peculiarity, we will be the single greatest nation on earth. This self-awareness of the Jews may not be unconnected with the tragic experiences of their past which dates back to Bible times and the more recent second world war.

This severe adversity that this particular set of people were subjected to made them more refined and resilient. What's more? They overcame and became bigger and better. It is like proving the truism true that 'What does not kill you makes you stronger'.

Adversity, challenges and crisis are good for a country. Adversity and crisis make a nation better and stronger. Why? Because bitter experiences make a nation or people to look inward and discover the virtues within them. When this virtues are discovered, they are then used as building blocks to build an indomitable nation. Therefore, we can safely establish at this point that a nation is built from the inwards and not outwards. What is required to build a nation is the virtues and potential within, it is not without. Nation building has nothing to do with anything external, political campaigns and foreign aids. Unfortunately, this is the focus of many governments and countries right now.

What is required to build Nigeria into the greatest country in the world is right within us. What we must do is turn the stones of our current adversity into the building blocks of a great nation. Out of the broken pieces and ruins, we can build an edifice.

To prove my point, I can tell you how the United States came out of the civil war to build themselves a strong nation. I can tell you how Germany came out of the ruins of the Second World War, and within fifty years, built themselves one of the strongest economies on earth. In same manner, Nigeria is going to rise from her current despair to become an enviable nation. Mark my words.

Why we Must Build a Nation

Do you notice my emphasis on the word nation all along?

I have deliberately used the word country sparingly so far, over and over again in this book. This is because a nation is quite different from a country. A country and a nation are not one and same words. They are totally different. What will you say differentiates a country from a nation? Let me explain to you.

A country according to the Webster dictionary is an indefinite, usually extended expanse of land, region or miles of open land. In other words, country often refers to the geographical space or land on which certain people live and are found. Nothing may be essentially peculiar about a country. Yet some are.

When we have to consider the peculiarity of a country and the peculiarity of Nigeria, you will agree with me that Nigeria is an extremely peculiar country. Nigeria as a country is peculiar in the sense of the vast and enormous amount of natural resources the land is blessed with. Apart from a year-long favorable weather, Nigeria boasts of having some of the rarest and most abundant forms of certain mineral resources. Among the mineral resources which are most abundant in Nigeria are Emerald, Tin, Marble, Granite, Tantalite/Columbite, Lead/Zinc, Barytes, Iron-ore, Kaolin, Cassiterite, Gold,

Dolomite, Bentonite, Phsochlore, Clay, Coal, Wolram, Salt, Bismuth, Fluoride, Molybdenite, Gemstone, Bauxite. This is aside the well-known Crude oil and agricultural products which Nigeria boasts. Nigeria as a country has one of the most abundant mineral deposits in the world in form of materials and farmland produce. This alone attests to the fact that Nigeria is one of the greatest countries in the world.

I could choose to dwell on the peculiarity of Nigeria as a country, I might still be able to show you why Nigeria is one of the greatest names in the world. However that is not my focus right now.

So what is Nigeria as a nation? A nation has been defined as a large body of people united by common descent, history, culture, or language, inhabiting a particular state or territory.

The major difference therefore between a nation and a country often border on unity and whether the citizens have bought into a common vision. This difference often marks the difference between poor countries and prosperous nations. The Jews for example have often been referred to as the Jewish nation.

Can you appreciate the difference right now between a nation and a country? While there are many countries in the world, not every one of them exist as a nation.

A nation is known by the unity that exists between its people, their history, their culture and language. The call for unity in all of the aforementioned means that there could be several cultures, many languages and different historical facts. However, a nation is born when a people decide to be united in spite of individual and slight differences. When the unity of purpose and common interest is placed above the differences of race, tribe or religion, then a nation is born.

Before any country can grow and develop on earth, they must first exist as a nation, as a single entity. This single entity existing in unity is absolute.

Yet, like I wrote earlier, there can only be a call for unity when there are different parts to a thing. So for example, there can only be call for unity in a country because it has many and different parts.

People have asked me over and again how we can best achieve unity for our country. My response to them is simple. The way to achieve unity is through vision. Uniformity is not necessarily unity, we all can exist as a tribe in the whole country, yet we may not still be united. But when there is a burning vision for the entire country, then a nation is born. We will be united by vision even though we have many languages, different tribes and different religions. This is why the first step to Nigeria's greatness is to first exist as a Nation through the path of vision and exist beyond being just a country.

You will notice that many of the greatest nations in the world have a vision that they are working towards. For example, a nation can decide to be among the top eight economies of the world within a certain time, they will achieve it if they plan and make every citizen buy into that vision. What that means is that when we exist as a nation, we can then pine a vision of becoming the greatest country in the world, and this will be so easy for us to achieve. The resources are there, we only need to agree to be united around a vision.

What Makes the Jews a Powerful Nation?

Let us for a moment go back to our discussion and illustration of the Jews. What I just explained in the above paragraphs explains why the Jewish nation is a strong nation. It explains the secret of the Jews.

The Jews are only about 16 million people altogether in the world. That population is just about 0.2% of the entire population of people on earth. Yet this small number of people are significant and form a formidable force wherever you find them. They are simply one of the greatest nations on earth currently. Like we also established earlier, their impact in the world cannot be unconnected with the tragedy that their forefathers were subjected to which has born within them what you can also call the Jewish spirit.

If we are to measure their impact in the world using the Nobel Prize, a set of annual international awards bestowed in a number of categories by Swedish and Norwegian institutions in recognition of academic, cultural, and/or scientific advances, the Jews have the highest number of awardees. This same feat, I see Nigeria achieving someday. I know you are quick to ask me how this will be done, that is why you have this book in your hands right now. Please read on.

The Nobel Prize has come to be accepted as the yard-stick for global excellence, innovation and ideas. This the Jews have also dominated. How many of this have they won?

At least 197 Jews and people of Jewish ancestry have been awarded the Nobel Prize, accounting for 22% of all individual recipients worldwide between 1901 and 2016.

This constitutes 36% of all US recipients during the same period.

In the scientific research fields of Chemistry, Economics, Physics, and Physiology/Medicine, the corresponding world percentage is 26%. Among women laureates in the four research fields, the Jewish percentage is 33%.

Of organizations awarded the Nobel Peace Prize, 22% were founded principally by Jews or by people of half-Jewish descent. Since the turn of the century (i.e., since the year 2000), Jews have been awarded 25% of all Nobel Prizes and 27% of those in the scientific research fields. (Jews currently make up approximately 0.2% of the world's population and 2% of the US population.)

In Chemistry, till date there are 36 prize winners, 21% of world total winners.

In Economics category, there are 30 prize winners of Jewish origin. They form 38% of world total winners and 50% of US total winners.

In Literature there are 15 prize winners who are Jews.

There are 9 Peace prize winners of Jewish origin.

In Physics, 52 prize winners are Jews, 26% of world total winners.

In Physiology or Medicine, there are 55 Jewish prize winners, which is 26% of the world total.

Nigeria till date has only 1 prize winner across all categories. There are 16 million Jews, and more than 180 million Nigerians. Though having same abilities, capabilities and spirit, why have the Jews achieved so much and Nigerians significantly less? Keep in mind that there is nothing the Jews have achieved that Nigeria as a nation cannot achieve in multiple fold, Nigeria is much more blessed than many of these nations.

Among the notable Jews you probably do not know are Albert Einstein, perhaps the most famous scientist of the 20th century. He proposed a groundbreaking theory of relativity (including his famous equation $e=mc^2$). Einstein's work established the foundation for much of modern physics and had a profound impact on everything from quantum theory to nuclear power and the atomic bomb.

Others include Karl Marx, the German philosopher, economist, and revolutionary, who wrote **"The Communist Manifesto"** and **"Das Kapital"**, with the help of Friedrich Engels. These works greatly influenced modern socialism and the social sciences. Marx is considered one of the founders of economic history and sociology.

Yet another notable Jew is Dr. Sigmund Freud, an Austrian physician. He was the founder of psychoanalysis and father of psychiatry. He theorized that the symptoms of hysterical patients represent forgotten and unresolved infantile psycho-sexual conflicts. His psychoanalytic theories profoundly influenced 20th-century thought.

Our mentions will not be complete without mentioning the likes of Dr. Jonas Salk, who created the first polio vaccine.

Dr. Abraham Waksman coined the term antibiotics.

Casmir Funk, a Polish Jew, pioneered a new field of medical research and coined the word "vitamins."

Dr. Simon Baruch performed the first successful operation for appendicitis.

Dr. Paul "**Magic Bullet**" Ehrlich won the Nobel Prize in 1908 for curing syphilis.

Dr. Abraham Jacobi is considered America's father of pediatrics.

Dr. Albert Sabin developed the first oral polio vaccine.

Haym Solomon and Isaac Moses are responsible for creating the first modern-banking institutions.

With all of these names I have included, I have not even done justice to up to 0.1% of what Jews have accomplished all around the world.

What am I saying? I have gone to that extent to show you what the Jewish spirit has done and is doing. That is the power of the spirit a nation possesses. When you have a nation with such an ideal, then the world beings to fear them, they simply stake awe into the minds of people around them. People fear them because they possess an innate spirit. This innate spirit is peculiar and borne out of the distinction of a nation. The Jews are one of such nations. Nigeria is one of such nations. There is nothing the Jews have done that Nigerians cannot march.

Nigerians can do More

This was my goal in writing this book and why you have this book in your hand right now. I have shown you what the Nigerian spirit is really made up of. Beyond that I have shown you what the Nigerian spirit can achieve. I have shown you why the already developed nations at the moment such as the United States, Germany, Great Britain and France are nothing compared to Nigeria. In fact like we already predicted, all of these nations will have to come to learn from Nigeria. Like we have seen through the pages of this book, Nigeria has the potential to become the greatest country in the world. The systems and steps have been well outlined so far.

So far, I have said things that I can see very clearly. In no distant time, though Nigeria was colonized by the British, the British will have to learn from Nigeria. I am saying with all audacity, that though Nigeria is currently being despised by the world, the time is near when this mighty nations will have to sit at the feet of Nigeria to learn a thing or two.

Just as the world cannot ignore the Jews, a people which form just about 0.25% of the entire population in the world, so also the world will not be able to ignore Nigeria. I am so sure because Nigeria has a peculiar fighting spirit. Like the Jews, Nigerians are indomitable, insuppressible, and extremely resilient. Nigerians are some of the most brilliant people you will find anywhere on the surface of the earth. Nigerians are simply unique. I am going to give you enough examples in a short while.

All of these is made possible by the power of our fighting spirit. Just like the Jews which I mentioned earlier who went through tough times to become one of the strongest nations on earth, only a few nations could have gone through what Nigerians have gone through and still be together.

In fact, the current existence of Nigeria today both as a country and as a nation is one that is still a mystery to many people. A lot of people cannot even understand it. Many have attributed it to a divine factor while some more people see it as mysterious. While all of that could be true, I see it as the peculiarity of Nigerians and the power of our spirit. It seems like Nigerians only bend, they don't break.

Now, when the capacity of our people is revealed, when all of these potentials of our people are maximized, when the prospects of Nigerians become glaring, when our promise and capabilities are finally fulfilled then the whole world will see that Nigerians can do no less than the Jews have been able to do. In fact, Nigeria will do in manifold what the Jews have done.

When the capacity, ability, power and aptitude of our people are manifested, when their talent and flair are discovered, harnessed and developed, imagine what we can do and what we will become. Imagine the force that Nigeria will become on earth with the power of our fighting spirit.

My assurance stems from my daily encounter with fellow Nigerians. It is rooted in the abilities of our people. It is based on my knowledge of the principles of the growth and development of Nations. Having been a consultant for many years to the governments of different countries, I can boldly declare that Nigeria can be the greatest nation on earth.

This is not just going to be in theory, now we are set as a people to make good our word. We are not just going to exist in our latent state, we are going to activate our ability and work out our potential. We are going to teach the world how a nation can rise quickly from the ocean of despair unto the pinnacle of greatness and accomplishment. We are set now to take our place in the comity of nations and to dominate and lead the world. This is simply our time, this is the time for Nigeria.

The Nigerian spirit is peculiar, the Nigerian ability is rare, there is only one kind of the Nigerian people you will see on the surface of the earth. I am not just saying this because I am a Nigerian, I am also saying this as a citizen of the world and as someone who has travelled to more than sixty countries and have met millions of people of diverse races, nations, religions and colors around the world. I am saying this because I have sat down to analyze and to discover, I have sat down to think and plan. I have proofs, I have facts. I have share a lot of that with you already in this rare form of book. I am coming out to say, Nigerians are peculiar and we have what it takes to teach not just America, but also the entire world.

Why Nigerians are 'Corrupt'

If you will permit me to say that many of the vices Nigerians are known for around the world today is also a function of the Nigerian Spirit. It is not possible for Nigerians to be in any environment or country and you will not know they exist even if they are five in number. You just must observe them, you just must notice them.

I have had encounters with many people over the years that without any introduction or any word from them, I have been forced to ask them 'Are you a Nigerian'. Often times than not, I have not been disappointed. Why? I could look at the way you speak, the force in your speech, your attitude to life, your work ethic, your approach to people, your attitude to disappointments and failure, your level of ambition and desire to achieve, your perspectives of hardship and tough times, and I may be able to tell to a larger degree whether you are a Nigerian or not or whether you have dwelt with Nigerians for so long.

Nigerians do not just struggle to be known, we do not just struggle to be heard, we do everything that is needed to achieve what we want to achieve. There is a natural dominating spirit that comes with being a Nigerian. Why? A function of the Nigerian spirit.

Please read this carefully now, I am just about to tell you something very important which will most likely blow your mind. I am saying that the vices often times that Nigerians are known for around the world is a function of the Nigerian spirit. The zeal, the passion, the dedication to be successful, the ambition, the goal-orientation of many young people which has pushed them into vices and wrong-doing must now be looked at in a new perspective. While I totally condemn all of the nefarious acts, I have critically examined the spirit from which it is coming from, the Nigerian spirit.

Now from my understanding of life, from what I have experimented with over the years, from the possibilities and the achievements that I have seen in Ukraine, a nation which I have lived for almost thirty years, from picking people off the streets and gutters, cleaning them, housing them, rehabilitating them till they are members of parliaments and successful politicians, from picking people who the society have given up on and raising them till they are successful global business men and millionaires, I have come to know and appreciate the power of the human potential.

My dear friend, the truth is that you cannot give up on anyone in life. I have seen countless cases. I have seen what people can do and become when you rehabilitate and believe in them. I have seen what gold lies in people when you polish them and clean them up. I have seen the beauty of the human spirit. I have come to see the treasure in a thief or a man who went to steal because he wants to provide for his household. When the entire world sees a thief, I see a caring father that lacks the right value system. When the entire world condemns him, I choose to lend him a hand and show to him what great things he could do with his life.

At the end of the day, you will only discover that everyone on earth only needs a little push, a little belief, a little instruction and they will become super stars and giants. This is my belief and that to which I have not just dedicated the course of my life to, but also the remainder of my life to. I belief in gold, and I also belief that gold will often come to you as dirt. So I believe in gold and the dirt that covers them. It takes understanding to see gold in dirt, while it is still dirt.

Let me share this example with you. My book Publishers have often complained to me about how many of my books are being pirated in Nigeria and how unauthorized copies are been sold everywhere. They see many fake copies of my books on the street, in markets, and illegal bookshops. Many times, they just want me to authorize them to begin the arrest of such people. In fact there was a time that the government caught certain people with a very large collection of my books which had been pirated and was being carried to a certain place, they called me and wanted to know what they should do with 'the thieves'.

My response to them was very shocking to them. Indeed my approach to such issues is shocking to a lot of people and I personally do not understand why they are not thinking the way I am thinking. What did I do? I immediately called my media team and I went on to broadcast and announce that if there is any pirate of my books who is listening to me, I want him to contact me to get the original copy. I told all the pirates that I want to work with them. Rather than endangering their own lives going about business the illegal way, I would like to empower them by authorizing them to use the original manuscript instead of the pirated ones. I will give them the permission to sell all the copies, keep all the money and make a life for themselves.

People were shocked to hear me say such a thing. Why did I say that? Now consider this with me, for a moment close your eyes to all the evil this men and women have done. Overlook for a moment their evil. Look at the ingenuity it takes to get copies of my books in Nigeria though I am in Ukraine, imagine what it takes to convince people and bookshops to buy such books. Selling an original copy of a book is tough enough, how much harder it is to sell a fake copy. Now this is what this people have been able to do. I am looking for such talents to work with, I am looking for such ambitious people, I am looking for these rogues, militants, armed robbers, prostitutes etc. I want to work with all of them. I love them and I appreciate the fighting spirit within them.

How to take Advantage of 'Our Corruption'

When we have this perspective of our people, it wouldn't take so long before we finally change our nation. When we look at things with a new eye, things will change. Rather than expecting everyone to change, if only we will be the one to change where we stand and hence our perspectives, we will change the world. We will make Nigeria the greatest country in the world.

What am I saying? I am saying that beyond the vices, there is a positive spirit that underlies the evil that people do, especially Nigerians. While we think of what to do to change the Nigerian evil doers, we ourselves must first change our perspective of their situation.

We can think on how to empower these people. We can think on how to open up opportunities for them. This is a major lesson we have learnt in this book.

This again is why I am convinced that Nigeria can be the greatest nation in the world. Note any country right now that is known significantly for crime, mark it down, if the eyes of such people will only be opened to their own beauty, they will know and understand that they can change the world. They can impact the world in a major, significant and positive way.

Building Nigeria's Path to Glory

Let us look at the example of the Jews again. The Jews as a nation have come to the awareness of the power they carry. They have come to appreciate their difference and significance, right from the family they have learnt to channel that focus and energy into the right things. Often times, they are hated and are severely attacked, but it doesn't matter, it only keeps making them stronger.

This is also the reason certain traditions are followed religiously in Jewish family. The Jews do not allow their children to go to just any form of school, they would rather set up their own communities and build their own schools. They would teach and inculcate certain values into their children from a young age. From young ages also, this Jewish children begin to impact the world in a significant way. This is what it means to appreciate your uniqueness and difference. This is what it takes to focus that spirit, that peculiar spirit, that national spirit into the right things and engagements to build a nation.

Now, the total Jewish population all around the world is not even up to the population of Lagos state in Nigeria. In other words, Lagos state Nigeria alone has the potential to out do everything that the Jews have done on earth if certain principles which I have taught in this book will be properly understood and applied.

If we will understand the power of the Nigerian spirit and the value of the Nigerian people, if we will understand and see the beauty of all the young men and women who daily constitute and pose challenges on the streets of Mushin, Ojuelegba, Ikorodu etc in Lagos, we will better understand how to help them actualize their potentials just like the Jews.

If we will begin to develop our own people, if we will follow the road map that I have helped you see in this book, what the Jews have done and achieved will seem like a child's play to what we will do and achieve. Nobody will be able to compare to Nigerians. In fact, all nations of the world will look at Nigeria and wonder. When we come to appreciate the value of men and women of Warri, if we will see the beauty of the creativity and the abilities of the people on the streets of Delta, if we will know the talents and the value that is buried in the crevices of the Onitsha market, we will begin to understand that no nation can compare to Nigeria on the surface of the earth.

Many people have often complained about the Almajiri children and the street children of the north. Many are calling for different ways to restrict their movement, many only look at how they are yearly recruited into the dreaded terrorist group, Boko Haram. Contrary to what many people see and are talking about, all I see in the Almajiri children is potential. I look at them and they are not any different from the children of New York, Amsterdam or Melbourne. In fact through this book, you can now see why I believe the Almajiri children are better than the children of New York. Now if you have read this book, you will know that I am not crazy. There is potential everywhere, if only we can see. When I look all around me in Nigeria, everywhere is filled with potential. The Nigerian Spirit is an advantage, it is not a curse.

Now you know that I have basis and grounds for my claim. Beyond claims however, I have given you facts and statistics. As a matter of fact, when I say that 'Nigeria can become the greatest country in the world, I am not just saying that Nigeria is going to attain something that is outside of her power, a good student of history will tell you that was the original position Nigeria was before. It is unfortunate that certain things happened, Nigeria lost ground and we are where we are today. The whole world however must know that Nigeria is coming back. We are rising and we will rise not just above America, but also the rest of the world.

NIGERIA SHALL INDEED ONE DAY TEACH THE WORLD.

Again in closing this book, let me repeat the quote from Jim Rohn. He seemed to have seen the future which I see for Nigeria. This is what he said:

> Let others lead small lives, but not you. Let others argue over small things, but not you. Let others cry over small hurts, but not you. Let others leave their future in someone else's hands, but not you.
>
> Jim Rohn

SO HELP US GOD!!!

For the love of God, Church and Nation
By Pastor Sunday Adelaja.

NUGGETS

- Nigeria is one of the most peculiar, distinct and enviable nations in the world.
- There are still so many millions of Sunday Adelajas wasting away in their villages and hamlets without any sort of recognition whatsoever.
- Imagine what awaits Nigeria when all our potential is harnessed towards the development of every Citizen, Nigeria, Africa and the world at large.
- Imagine what will happen to Nigeria when the genius in every child is unlocked.
- There is a grand design to start multiple Universities in my lifetime of which the University of Life has begun and is running adequately.
- The Nigeria Transformation project is here for good. Together we will build Nigeria and make it the greatest country in the world.
- My story strongly proves that every child has hope. Every child has a destiny him. Every child is a star.
- Nigeria is going to rise from her current despair to become an enviable nation. Mark my words.
- Before any country can grow and develop on earth, they must first exist as a nation, as a single entity.

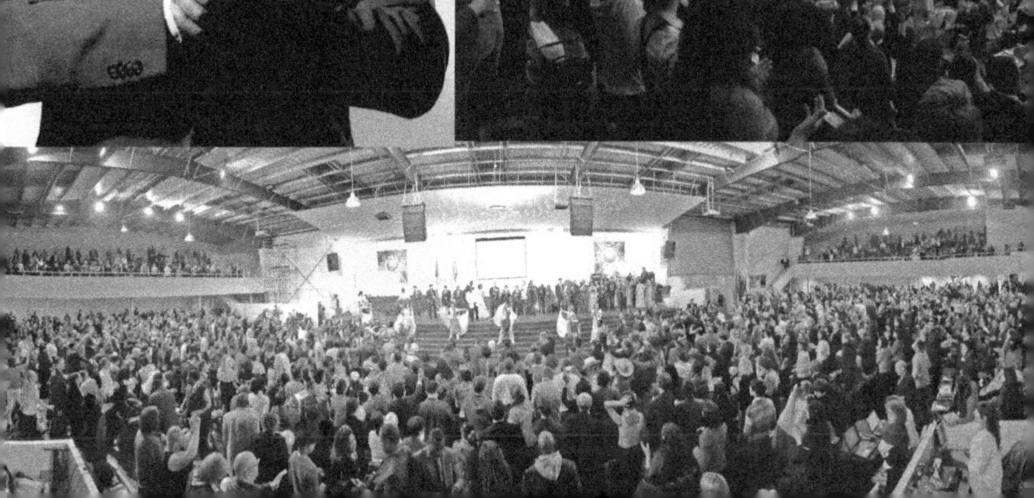

SUNDAY ADELAJA'S BIOGRAPHY

Pastor Sunday Adelaja is the Founder and Senior Pastor of The Embassy of the Blessed Kingdom of God for All Nations Church in Kyiv, Ukraine.

Sunday Adelaja is a Nigerian-born Leader, Thinker, Philosopher, Transformation Strategist, Pastor, Author and Innovator who lives in Kiev, Ukraine.

At 19, he won a scholarship to study in the former Soviet Union. He completed his master's program in Belorussia State University with distinction in journalism.

At 33, he had built the largest evangelical church in Europe — The Embassy of the Blessed Kingdom of God for All Nations.

Sunday Adelaja is one of the few individuals in our world who has been privileged to speak in the United Nations, Israeli Parliament, Japanese Parliament and the United States Senate.

The movement he pioneered has been instrumental in reshaping lives of people in the Ukraine, Russia and about 50 other nations where he has his branches.

His congregation, which consists of ninety-nine percent white Europeans, is a cross-cultural model of the church for the 21st century.

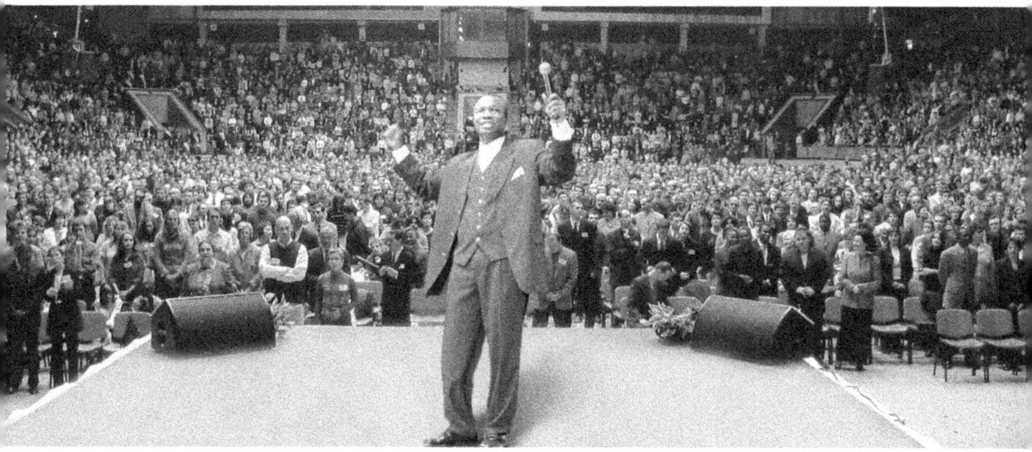

His life mission is to advance the Kingdom of God on earth by raising a generation of history makers who will live for a cause larger, bigger and greater than themselves. Those who will live like Jesus and transform every sphere of the society in every nation as a model of the Kingdom of God on earth.

His economic empowerment program has succeeded in raising over 200 millionaires in the short period of three years.

Sunday Adelaja is the author of over 300 books, many of which are translated into several languages including Russian, English, French, Chinese, German, etc.

His work has been widely reported by world media outlets such as The Washington Post, The Wall Street Journal, New York Times, Forbes, Associated Press, Reuters, CNN, BBC, German, Dutch and French national television stations.

Pastor Sunday is happily married to his "Princess" Bose Dere-Adelaja. They are blessed with three children: Perez, Zoe and Pearl.

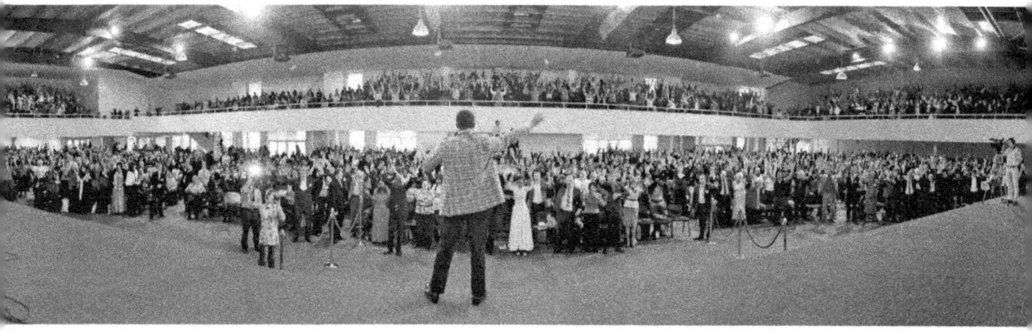

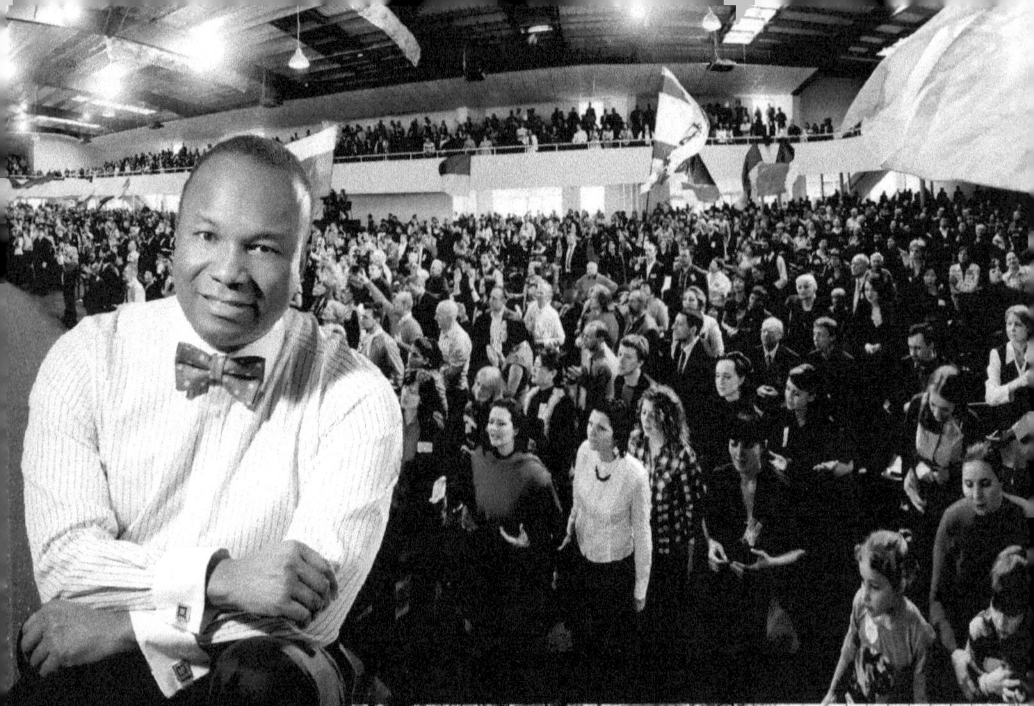

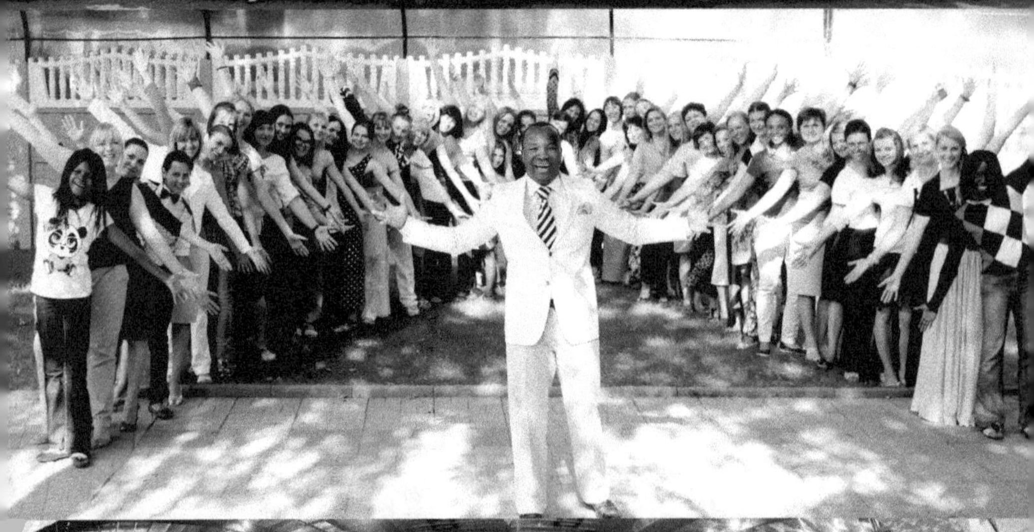

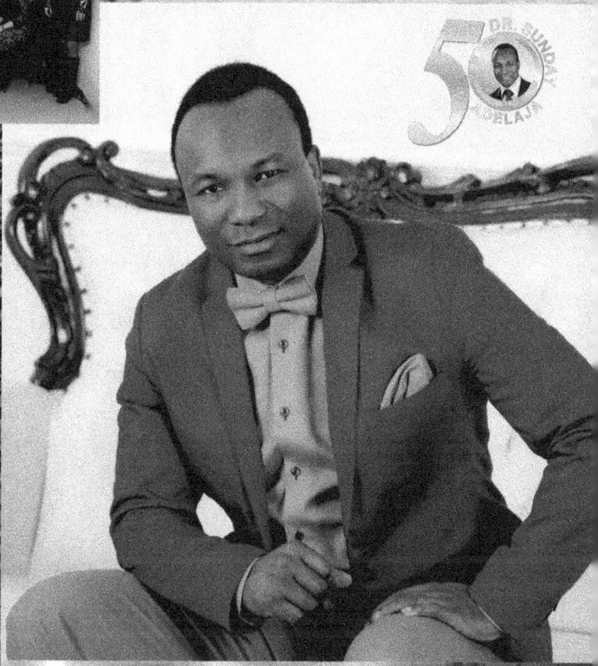
50
DR. SUNDAY
ADELAJA

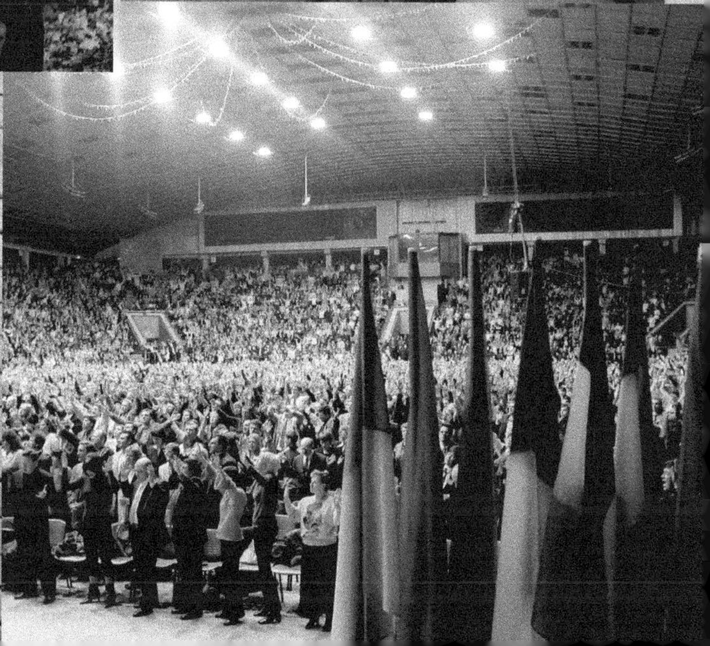

Bill Clinton —
42[Nd] President Of The United States (1993–2001), Former Arcansas State Governor

Ariel "Arik" Sharon —
Israeli Politician, Israeli Prime Minister (2001–2006)

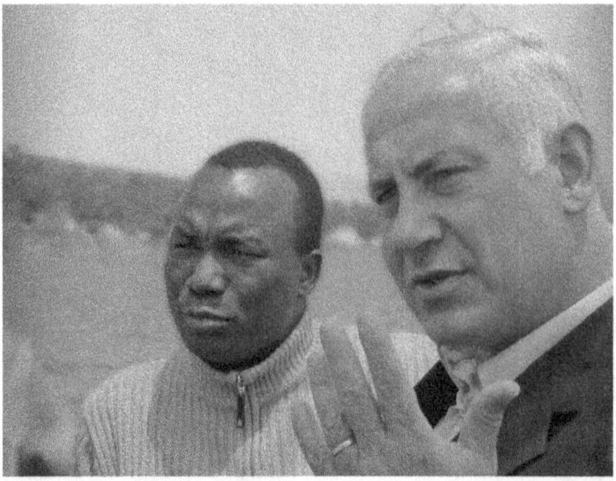

Benjamin Netanyahu —
Statesman Of Israel. Israeli Prime Minister (1996–1999), Acting Prime Minister (From 2009)

Jean ChrEtien —
Canadian Politician, 20Th Prime Minister Of Canada, Minister Of Justice Of Canada, Head Of Liberan Party Of Canada

Rudolph Giuliani —
American Political Actor, Mayor Of New York Served From 1994 To 2001. Actor Of Republican Party

Colin Powell —
Is An American Statesman And A Retired Four-Star General In The Us Army, 65Th United States Secretary Of State

Peter J. Daniels — Is A Well-Known And Respected Australian Christian International Business Statesman Of Substance

Madeleine Korbel Albright — An American Politician And Diplomat, 64Th United States Secretary Of State

Kenneth Robert Livingstone — An English Politician, 1St Mayor Of London (4 May 2000 – 4 May 2008), Labour Party Representative

Sir Richard Charles Nicholas Branson —
English Business Magnate, Investor And Philanthropist. He Founded The *Virgin Group*, Which Controls More Than 400 Companies

Mel Gibson —
American Actor And Filmmaker

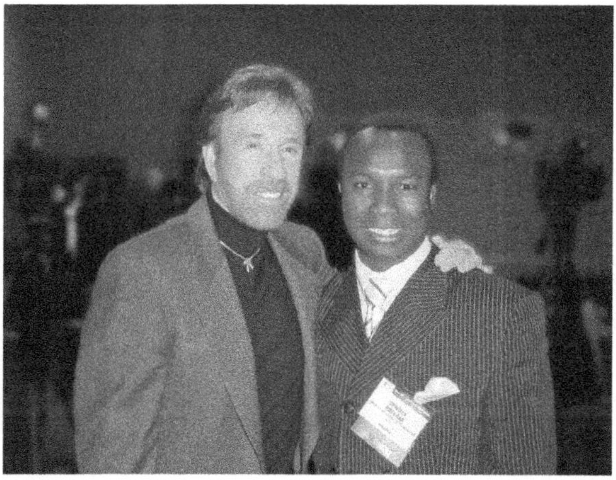

Chuck Norris —
American Martial Artist, Actor, Film Producer And Screenwriter

Christopher Tucker — American Actor And Comedian

Bernice Albertine King — American Minister Best Known As The Youngest Child Of Civil Rights Leaders Martin Luther King Jr. And Coretta Scott King Andrew

Andrew Young — American Politician, Diplomat, And Activist, 14Th United States Ambassador To The United Nations, 55Th Mayor Of Atlanta

General Wesley
Kanne Clark —
4-Star General And Nato
Supreme Allied Commander

Dr. Sunday Adelaja's family:
Perez, Pearl, Zoe and Pastor Bose Adelaja

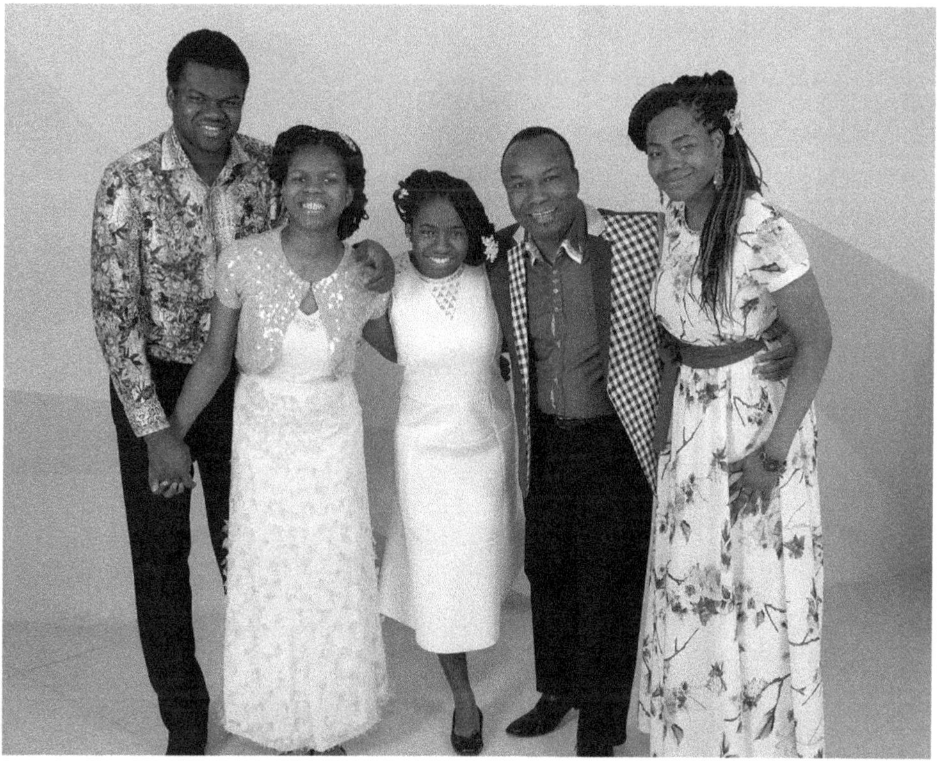

FOLLOW
SUNDAY ADELAJA
ON SOCIAL MEDIA

Subscribe And Read Pastor Sunday's Blog:

www.sundayadelajablog.com

Follow these links and listen to over 200 of Pastor Sunday`s Messages free of charge:

http://sundayadelajablog.com/content/

Follow Pastor Sunday on Twitter:

www.twitter.com/official_pastor

Join Pastor Sunday's Facebook page to stay in touch:

www.facebook.com/pastor.sunday.adelaja

Visit our websites for more information about Pastor Sunday's ministry:

http://www.godembassy.com

http://www.pastorsunday.com

http://sundayadelaja.de

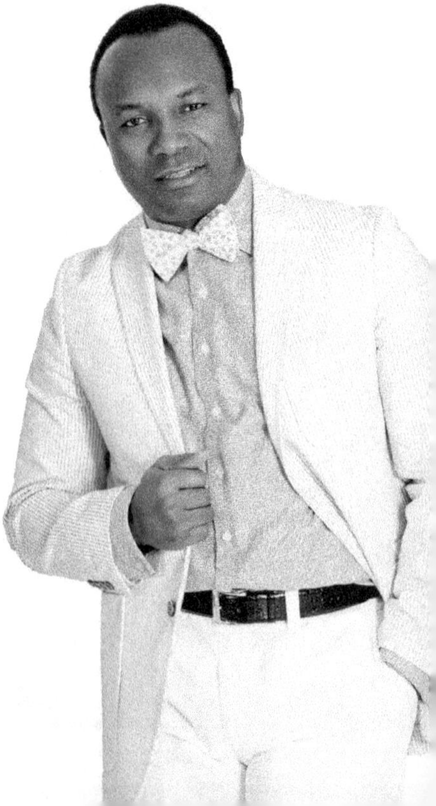

CONTACT

FOR DISTRIBUTION OR TO ORDER
BULK COPIES OF THIS BOOK,
PLEASE CONTACT US:

USA

CORNERSTONE PUBLISHING

info@thecornerstonepublishers.com

+1 (516) 547-4999

www.thecornerstonepublishers.com

AFRICA

SUNDAY ADELAJA MEDIA LTD.

E-mail: btawolana@hotmail.com

+2348187518530, +2348097721451, +2348034093699

LONDON, UK

PASTOR ABRAHAM GREAT

abrahamagreat@gmail.com

+447711399828, +441908538141

KIEV, UKRAINE

pa@godembassy.org

Mobile: +380674401958

Best Selling Books by Dr. Sunday Adelaja
Available on Amazon.com and Okadabooks.com

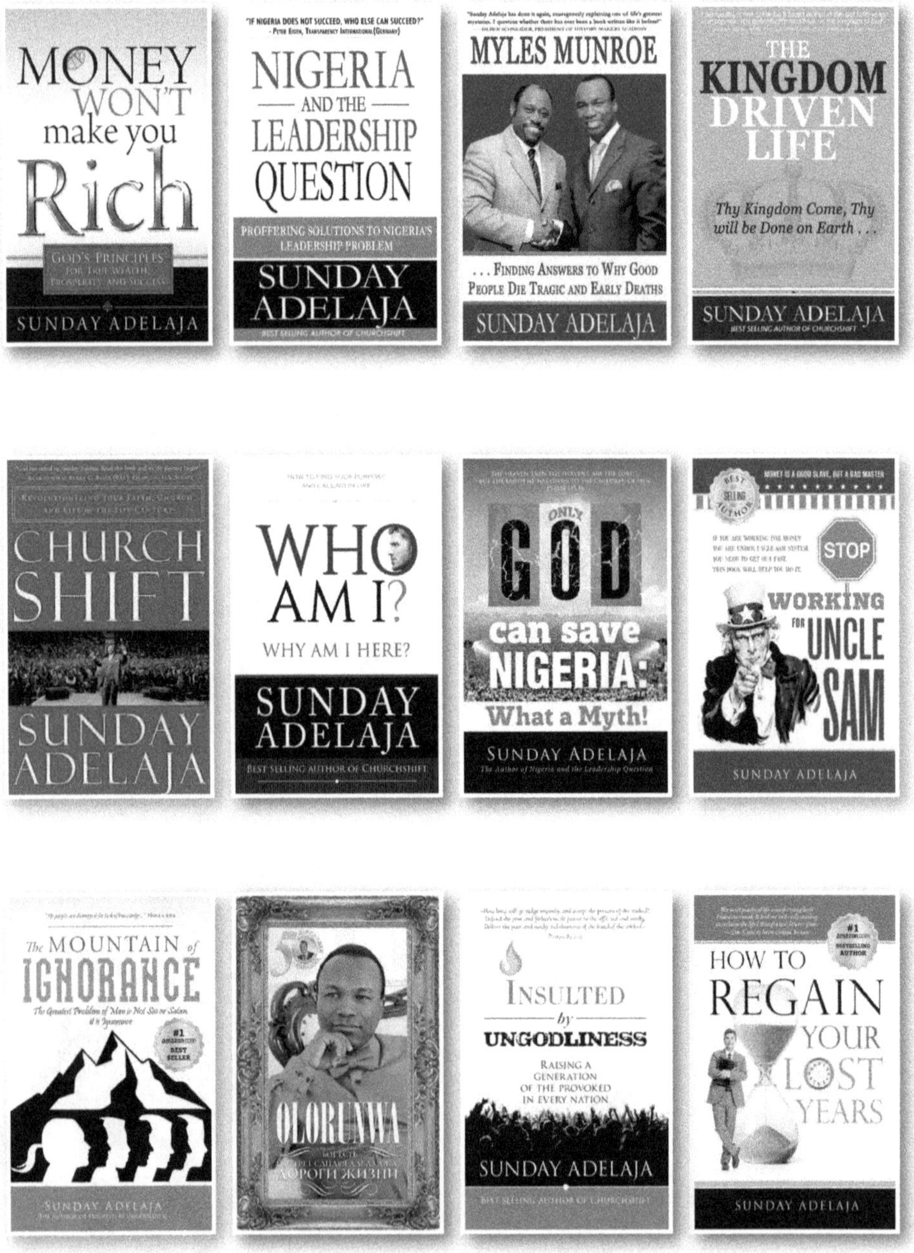

Best Selling Books by Dr. Sunday Adelaja
Available on Amazon.com and Okadabooks.com

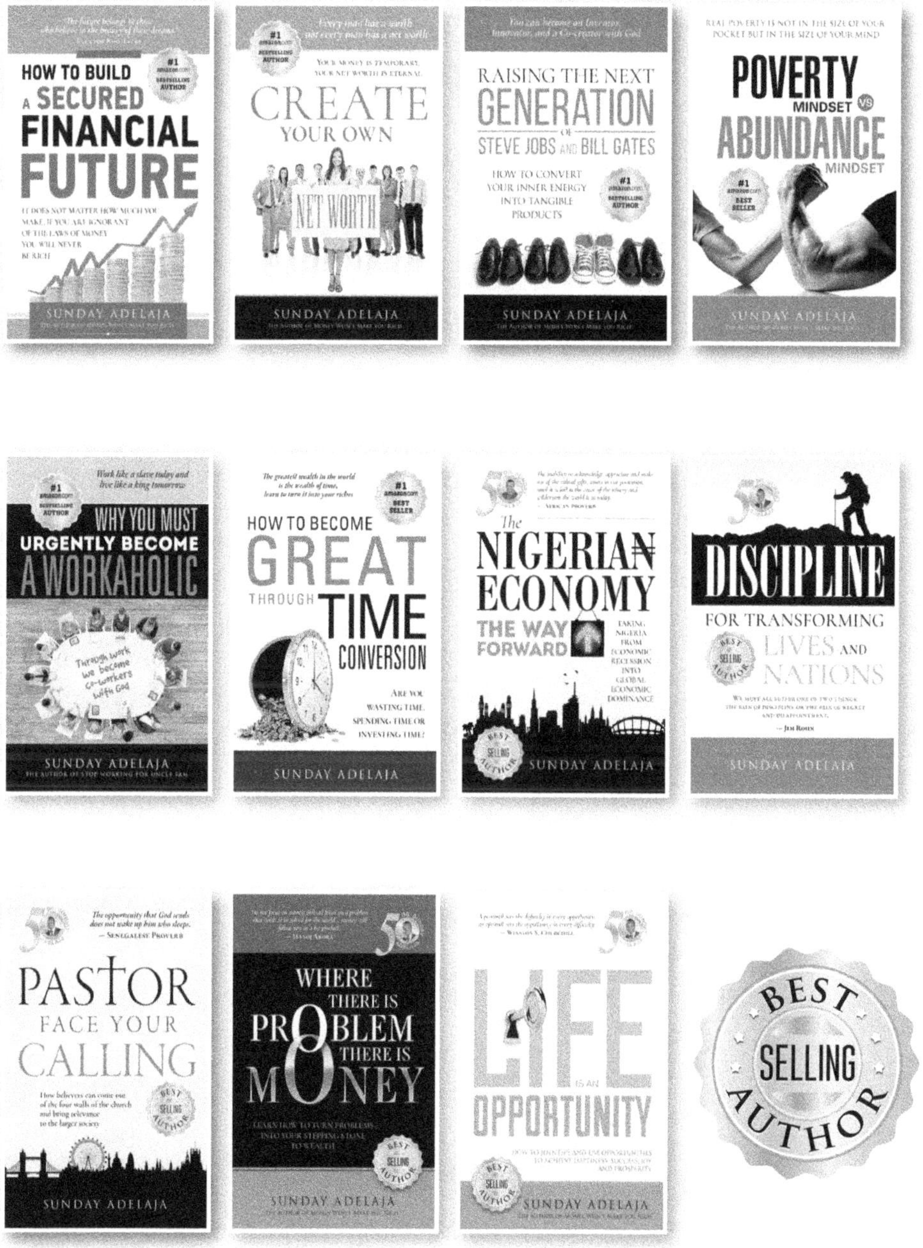

Golden Jubilee Series Books
by Dr. Sunday Adelaja

1. Who Am I
2. Only God Can Save Nigeria
3. The Mountain Of Ignorance
4. Stop Working For Uncle Sam
5. Poverty Mindset Vs Abundance Mindset
6. Raising The Next Generation Of Steve Jobs And Bill Gates
7. How To Build A Secured Financial Future
8. How To Become Great Through Time Conversion
9. Create Your Own Net Worth
10. Why You Must Urgently Become A Workaholic
11. How To Regain Your Lost Years
12. Pastor, Face Your Calling
13. Discipline For Transforming Lives And Nations
14. Excellence Your Key To Elevation
15. No One Is Better Than You
16. Problems Your Shortcut To Prominence
17. Let Heroes Arise!
18. How To Live An Effective Life
19. How To Win In Life
20. The Creative And Innovative Power Of A Genius
21. The Veritable Source Of Energy
22. The Nigerian Economy. The Way Forward
23. How To Get What You Need In Life
24. 7 Tips To Self-Fulfillment
25. Life Is An Opportunity
26. The Essence And Value Of Life
27. A Visionless Life Is A Meaningless Life
28. Where There Is Problem There Is Money
29. Work Is Better Than Vacation, Labour Better Than Favour
30. How To Overcome The Fear Of Death
31. Discovering The Purpose And Calling Of Nations
32. How To Become A Developed Nation Throught The Dignity Of Labor
33. Your Greatnes Is Proportional
34. Why Losing Your Job Is The Best Thing That Could Happen To You
35. What Do You Do With Your Time
36. Life Is Predictable
37. How To Be In The Here And Now
38. I Am A Person. Am I A Personality?
39. Discover The Source Of Your Latent Energy
40. How To Form Value Systems In A Child
41. Why I Am Unlucky
42. Hello! I Am Searching For Problems
43. Holistic Personality
44. How To transform And Build a Civilized Nation
45. Could You Be The Abraham Of Your Nation
46. The teambuilding skills of Jesus
47. How to keep your focus
48. The sin of irresponsibility
49. How Africans Brought Civilization To Europe
50. The Danger Of Monoculturalism

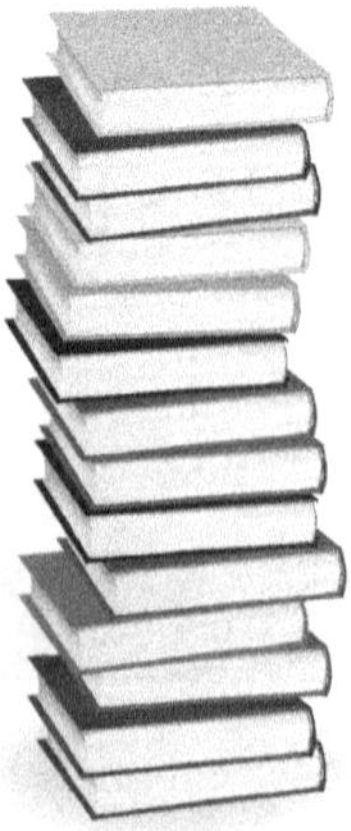

FOR DISTRIBUTION OR TO ORDER BULK COPIES OF THIS BOOKS, PLEASE CONTACT US:

USA | CORNERSTONE PUBLISHING
E-mail: info@thecornerstonepublishers.com, +1 (516) 547-4999
www.thecornerstonepublishers.com

AFRICA | SUNDAY ADELAJA MEDIA LTD.
E-mail: btawolana@hotmail.com
+2348187518530, +2348097721451, +2348034093699

LONDON, UK | PASTOR ABRAHAM GREAT
E-mail: abrahamagreat@gmail.com, +447711399828, +441908538141

KIEV, UKRAINE |
E-mail: pa@godembassy.org, Mobile: +380674401958

www.ingramcontent.com/pod-product-compliance
Lightning Source LLC
Chambersburg PA
CBHW022054210326
41519CB00054B/379
* 9 7 8 1 9 0 8 0 4 0 8 7 9 *